How JINNAH
LIBERATED INDIA

Khurram Ali Shafique

Libredux

How Jinnah Liberated India
http://www.marghdeen.com
https://www.youtube.com/c/KhurramsDesk
www.facebook.com/Khurram.Ali.Shafique
https://twitter.com/khurramsdesk

First published in the United Kingdom in December 2022 by
Libredux Publishing, Nottingham.
http://www.libredux.com

ISBN: 978-1-9164516-2-9

The author gratefully acknowledges the support offered by
Allied Marketing (Pvt) Ltd, Pakistan
https://www.alliedmarketing.com.pk
in the publishing of this book.

Cover concept by Khurram Ali Shafique, inspired by a vintage
advertisement of the Pakistani movie *Armaan* (1966),
with input from Rabbia Javaid. Design layout,
and photo editing and colourisation by Saleena Karim.
Cover photographs © 2022 Libredux

To

The Soul of All Human Beings

Contents

Introduction

It's a mad, mad, mad, mad world we live in, because the loss of history does to societies what the loss of sanity may do to an individual.

The world today has no recollection of how the British Empire came to an end less than eighty years ago. Facts surrounding the independence of India, which brought the end of the British Empire in 1947, have long been replaced with myths and conspiracy theories. Since the British Empire was the greatest empire in the history of humankind, its rise and fall was bound to affect almost every nation of the world either directly or indirectly. Forgetting the facts about such an event is a loss of world history – a loss of the history of almost every nation of the world.

The result is what we see today: a world that seems to have gone mad, societies that are losing their best traits, and individuals who are finding it increasingly more difficult to relate to their societies or to each other.

This book aims to set this right. It is not only an account of how India gained independence, but also a recollection of what the people knew about it at that time, how they felt about it and what they hoped to get out of it. The book does not present things the way I want to see them. It presents things the way the people saw them as they happened at the time.

It gives me great pleasure to associate this book with the 125th anniversary of Allied Marketing (Pvt) Ltd, Pakistan (website: alliedmarketing.com.pk), an associate company of S. M. Ilyas & Sons Ltd. Today a leading distributor of global brands, the enterprise started in 1898 out of a shop in the inner city of Lahore. Its founders represented exactly the type of hard work, commitment and entrepreneurship that was among the portents of that reawakening of the

South Asian society whose political aspects form the subject of this book.

I would like to thank everyone who has helped me and encouraged me in the writing of this book. On the professional side, I am indebted to the valuable advice provided by Saleena Karim as one of the finest authorities on the life and work of Quaid-i-Azam Muhammad Ali Jinnah.

I do not want to prolong this Introduction, since I would like the reader to get straight to starting the book. I would just like to say that I hope this book will help begin a process of relearning about our world. More about my work can be found at my website, Marghdeen.com; and my YouTube channel, Khurramsdesk. A complete biography of Jinnah from the point of view presented in this book is also available on that channel by the title, *Jinnah: A True Story* (2020).

1. The sideshow of Gandhi

On 20 February 1947, the British Prime Minister Clement Richard Attlee informed the House of Commons that the British were finally going to leave India no later than June 1948 (in the end they left much sooner, as we know). Of course, they had been saying for more than a hundred years that India would become independent *eventually*, but in the past, they had never said when. This time, they did.

The announcement surprised and shocked many. Less than three months earlier, the largest political party of British India, the Indian National Congress, had tacitly agreed to keep British presence in India for an indefinite period.

The British set up a Constituent Assembly in Delhi, and in theory this assembly was supposed to prepare a draft constitution for an India that was going to be ruled by its own people.

Once completed, the constitution was to be submitted to the British parliament. After (and if) the parliament approved it, and after it had received the royal assent, the constitution was to be implemented in the Indian Subcontinent *by the British*. Once (and if) it was implemented, hopefully the British would leave India, and India would become independent.

Even without the 'ifs' involved here, the process was going to be long-winded and time-consuming. The existing constitution of India, the Government of India Act 1935, had taken a little longer than seven years in the drafting and had covered much less ground than the new constitution was supposed to cover. More significantly, it had never become possible to implement the federal part of that constitution, and it was the federal part of the future constitution that could make India independent, *if* it got implemented.

If the previous constitution had taken seven years in the drafting and had defied implementation even twelve years later, how long would the proposed new constitution take for drafting and implementation? Seven plus twelve, nineteen years? Maybe more? Maybe less?

That did not matter to the Congress, which had taken the reins of the assembly on 9 December 1946, only two months and eleven days before the bombshell announcement by the British Prime Minister on 20 February 1947.

So, why did the British change their minds and decide to quit? The statement of the British Prime Minister suggests that it was not because of the Congress, but because of the other significant party: The All-India Muslim League.[1]

The League represented the Muslims, who comprised almost one-third of the population of British India. The League had secured almost 87 percent of all the seats reserved for the Muslims in the provincial and central legislatures of the country. Those legislatures later elected the members of the constituent assembly, and so the League secured 73 out of the 76 seats reserved for Muslims in that assembly – all except three.

The League had also made it clear that it would not join the assembly, since it demanded a separate assembly for the Muslim majority zones of the Subcontinent (the proposed state of 'Pakistan', at that time intended to include the territories now known as Pakistan and Bangladesh). Unlike the Congress, which had taken so many U-turns in the previous twenty-seven years

---

[1] As will be seen in the quote a few paragraphs later in the chapter, the statement mentions that 'differences among Indian Parties' were 'preventing the Constituent Assembly from functioning as it was intended that it should'. This was clearly understood as a reference to the boycott of the Assembly by the Muslim League. The draft statement originally considered by the British cabinet on 20-22 December actually started with the following words: 'His Majesty's Government greatly regret that it has not yet proved possible to bring within the Constituent Assembly in India all the major sections of Indian opinion and that the Muslim League, in particular, still find themselves unable to join in its deliberations.' Nicholas Mansergh *et al.* (ed.), *The Transfer of Power,* Vol.9, p.393

that it had been practically circling a roundabout since 1920, the League did just what it had said it would do.

The boycott of the constituent assembly by the League also precipitated a civil unrest already prevailing in British India. This boycott was the sole reason for the British decision to quit India, as the Prime Minister suggested in his announcement in the House of Commons on 20 February 1947:

> It is with great regret that His Majesty's Government find that there are still differences among Indian Parties which are preventing the Constituent Assembly from functioning as it was intended that it should... The present state of uncertainty is fraught with danger and cannot be indefinitely prolonged. His Majesty's Government wish to make it clear that it is their definite intention to take the necessary steps to effect the transference of power into responsible Indian hands by a date not later than June, 1948.[1]

The House of Lords considered adopting a resolution to 'dissociate themselves from the Government's declaration' but dropped it after a heated debate.[2] 'A correspondent lately returned from India' wrote in the journal *Round Table:*

> In the past, overseas empires have been abandoned, like that of Rome, because of pressure nearer home; or, as with Spain, by reason of exhaustion; or, as with the Axis Powers, as a result of ruinous defeat in war. None of these episodes furnishes any parallel to the policy of February 20; for that policy involved deliberate surrender of

---

[1] The statement appears in the British Parliamentary Debates [Hansard], 20 February 1947, House of Commons, Vol.433, cols.1396-1404; Waheed Ahmad (ed.), *The Nation's Voice,* Vol.5, pp.1105-1108. On the official website, https://hansard.parliament.uk, the debate appears as dated 10 February 1947, which is a mistake (retrieved 19 August 2022).

[2] On 25 and 26 February 1947; see transcript at https://hansard.parliament.uk (retrieved 19 August 2022)

authority by a ruling power which had just emerged victorious from the second world war, with its military capacity and prestige higher than ever.[1]

If there was one man who was not surprised by the British decision to quit India, it was Muhammad Ali Jinnah, popularly called the Quaid-i-Azam ('the Great Leader').

Jinnah was the president of the League, and the Sherlock Holmes of politics. In more than forty years of his political career, he had seldom made a promise he could not keep. This could have been partly because his training as a barrister had taught him how to choose words carefully, and partly due to his formidable insight into everything political.

Just a little more than two years earlier, on 16 January 1945, Jinnah had said to the Muslims, 'For twenty-five years, Mr. Gandhi had his way. Give me a way for two years and follow me.'[2] The Muslims followed him as he had asked, and the announcement that the British were quitting India came as had been promised by Jinnah – just two years, one month and four days after his statement.

It was not as if he had made his promise after arriving at some prior understanding with the British. He had also made another prophecy, one that was beyond the power of the British to fulfil. He had said, 'If British Government announced its intention of setting up Pakistan and Hindustan, Congress and Hindus would accept it within three months. In other words, the Government would have called the Congress bluff.'[3]

This also came true just as predicted. The announcement made by the British Prime Minister on 20 February 1947 indicated a readiness to concede the creation of Pakistan. The Congress, which had been opposing the idea all along,

---

[1] 'Deathbed of the Indian Empire' by 'a correspondent lately returned from India', *The Round Table* (1947), Vol. 37; no.147, p.231

[2] 16 January 1945; Khurshid Ahmad Khan Yusufi (ed.), *Speeches, Statements and Messages of the Quaid-e-Azam*, p.1981

[3] 29 February 1944; , *op. cit.* p.1838

announced its acceptance on 3 June 1947 – just three and a half months after the British announcement of 20 February 1947.

How Jinnah Liberated India therefore, is the question that should have been discussed thoroughly during the last seventy-five years, so that we could discover a new branch in the social sciences – including a new political science – for solving our problems effectively. The British Empire was the greatest empire of history, and Jinnah had defeated it without having a single soldier under his command. By studying his methods carefully enough, we might even have been able to make wars redundant by now.

Yet in all the discussions about the independence of India that have been done to death, the one question that has never been asked is, *How Jinnah Liberated India?* It has not been asked because the facts related to the independence of India have long been replaced by false theories, such as that Gandhi, Nehru or other Indian nationalists of the era were responsible for forcing the British to quit India; or that the British left India due to some ulterior motive; and so on. Let's get rid of those fallacies before proceeding with the main topic of this book.

2

Mohandas Karamchand Gandhi, known as 'Mahatma' (the Great Soul) among his followers, had spent most of his adult life in South Africa before returning to India in 1915 at the age of 45. He became prominent in the Indian politics three years later.

The weird thing about the campaigns he subsequently carried out in the name of independence is that their outcomes were *always* favourable to the British rather than the Indians:

1. While introducing the India Act 1919, which fell short of the Indian expectations for self-rule, the British had

promised that the Act would last only for ten years, and India would receive full independence within the Commonwealth afterwards. Gandhi rejected this, demanded and prophesied self-rule within a year, launched a civil disobedience movement for that purpose in 1920 and called it off less than two years later. The Act remained in effect for sixteen years instead of ten, and some parts of it remained effective until the very end of British rule.

2. The British offered to consult the Indian leaders during the preparation of the next constitution through a round table conference in 1930. Gandhi demanded that India be made independent immediately without any round table conference, and launched another movement of civil disobedience which lasted from 1930 to 1931. As before, the movement of Gandhi did not alter the course of things: Three round table conferences took place, one with the participation of Gandhi, and the proposed constitution came to effect in 1935.

3. In 1932, Gandhi launched his third movement, repeating the same demand, and again abandoning the movement without altering the course of things.

4. In 1942, the British offered to share power with Indians during the Second World War and to set up a constituent assembly of Indian representatives after the war. Gandhi refused to wait that long, demanded the immediate departure of the British, and launched his much-hyped 'Quit India' movement. The proposed assembly was set up after the end of the war, just as the British had originally intended, and received the full blessings of Gandhi (this is the assembly mentioned in the historic statement of Attlee, the assembly that the Muslim League had refused to join). The Congress did not get to share power with the British during the war, and instead almost all its leaders remained in jail until the end of the

war (and after the war the Congress accepted the same share in power that it had refused in 1942).

The following table summarizes these four episodes of the so-called political career of Gandhi.

YEAR(S)	BRITISH OFFER	GANDHI'S DEMAND	OUTCOME
1920 to 1922	India Act to last for 10 years; self-government afterwards	Independence for India within a year.	India Act lasted 16 years (some parts lasted longer); no self-government afterwards
1930 to 1931	Round Table Conference of Indian leaders to decide a new constitution.	Immediate independence for India, and no Round Table Conference.	Round Table Conference held three times, once with participation of Gandhi.
1932	Same as above.	Immediate independence for India.	Same as above.
1942 to 1945	Representative Constituent Assembly up after WW2, and Indian control of several departments of government during WW2.	Immediate independence for India ('Quit India' now, and not after WW2).	Representative Constituent Assembly after WW2 (with participation of Congress), but no Congress control of any department of government during WW2.

This comparison between the purported aim of each countrywide campaign and its actual outcome should be sufficient to show that Gandhi was nothing more than the longest running reality show of that era, and he might have played as much of a role in the Indian struggle for independence as *Hell's Kitchen* played in shaping the policies of the American government in the War Against Terror.

3

So, Gandhi was whistling in the wind the whole time, but why? This question was answered at the very outset by one of the most credible personalities in British India, Surendranath Banerjea – a veteran of the old guard of the Congress and one of the pioneers of the Indian independence movement. According to Banerjea, the tactics of Gandhi were meant to *keep* the British in India and *delay* its independence.

Referring to a pro-Indian newspaper of Britain, Banerjea said in December 1918, 'The *Manchester Guardian* complains that the extremists are playing into the hands of Lord Sydenham and his party and, by adding to the difficulties of the Government, may make it reluctant to proceed with the reforms at all.'[1] Lord Sydenham was a former governor of Bombay, well-known for his imperialistic policies. By 'extremists', Banerjea meant a particular segment of the Congress that had long been known by this name, and which had rallied round Gandhi at that time.

By 1930, when Gandhi started his second countrywide campaign, these extremists had taken control of the Hindu society almost completely. Dr Sir Muhammad Iqbal, the leading visionary

---

[1] Presidential address delivered by Banerjea on 1 November 1918; All-India Conference of the Moderate Party, *Report of the Proceedings of the First Session,* p.41

and political leader among the Muslims of India, observed 'a kind of understanding between Hindu India and British Imperialism— you perpetuate me in India, and I in return give you a Hindu oligarchy to keep all other Indian communities in perpetual subjection.'[1] Three years later, Iqbal commented that Hindu India had adopted a policy to give itself 'the permanent position of an agent of British imperialism in the East.'[2]

Therefore, when Jinnah presented a case for Pakistan in 1940, one of his key arguments was that the Hindu leaders of the times, led by Gandhi, 'wanted the British in this country, though that was not their official policy.'[3]

The 'Quit India' Movement launched by Gandhi in 1942 was a hoax, according to Jinnah. 'I refuse to believe that Mr. Gandhi thinks for a moment that the British would withdraw immediately at his request,' he said.[4] He repeated the deduction he had made about the Congress on a previous occasion:

> We know why they have launched the civil disobedience movement. The British government know why. It is to coerce the British Government to recognize the Congress as the only authoritative and representative organization of the people of India. The Congress says: 'Come to settlement with us. We are your friends; we desire to maintain your supremacy in this country. Come to terms with us and ignore the Mussalmans and other minorities.'[5]

The allegation raised by Jinnah was so well-known at that time that even the white paper on the Quit India movement published by the British Government of India in 1943 recorded it as 'a

---

[1] Presidential address delivered at the Allahabad session of the All-India Muslim League on 29 December 1930; Latif Ahmad Sherwani, *Speeches, Writings and Statements of Iqbal*, pp.16-17
[2] Statement issued on 6th December, 1933; *ibid*, p.290
[3] 24 January 1943; Yusufi (ed.), *Speeches, Statements and Messages of the Quaid-e-Azam*, p.1668
[4] 30 July 1942; *ibid*, pp.1593-1594
[5] Delhi, 30 November 1940; *ibid*, p.1281

view held, significantly, by the Muslim League and the Muslims in general.'[1]

4

The theory that the partition of India was a British conspiracy doesn't hold water in light of two facts that nobody can deny.

Firstly, the partition of India had been voted for by 75 percent of all the Muslims who went to the polls during the preceding election (and it did not matter that the election was not conducted on the basis of universal adult franchise, as we shall see shortly). Those votes translated to 100 percent of the seats reserved for the Muslims in the central legislature and in some of the provinces, and more than 80 percent in the legislatures of every other province except one – almost 87 per cent of all the seats reserved for the Muslims in all the legislatures across British India. These included provinces that were going to remain in India after the partition.

To suggest that such a high percentage of an entire electorate voted in favour of a foreign conspiracy to destroy their own country is to take away the very premise of democracy for any part of human race anywhere in the world. The following table illustrates the support which the idea of partition received in the election of 1945-1946.

LEGISLATURE	TOTAL SEATS FOR MUSLIMS	WON BY MUSLIM LEAGUE	%
Central	30	30	100
Assam	34	31	91

---

[1] Govt. of India, *Congress Responsibility for the Disturbance 1942-43,* p.11

Legislature	Total seats for Muslims	Won by Muslim League	%
Bengal	122	116	95.8
Bihar	40	34	85
Bombay	30	30	100
C. P. Berar	14	13	93
Madras	28	28	100
N.W.F.P.	38	17	45
Orissa	4	4	100
Punjab	88	79	89.3
Sindh	34	28	82
U.P.	66	54	82
Total	524	453	86.45
75% of all the votes cast by the Muslims were in favour of the Muslim League			

What Nazi propaganda did to the Jews in Germany is what happens to the Muslims living in India today whenever it is said that the partition of India was a British conspiracy. It amounts to saying that almost all the ancestors of the Muslims who now live in India were collaborators in a foreign conspiracy that was carried out through 80 to 100 percent of their elected representatives. It takes away human dignity from every Muslim of present-day India, and brands every child born to a Muslim in that country a traitor upon birth, condemned to remain guilty until proven innocent.

It hardly matters that not every adult was entitled to vote in 1946, and the franchise was restricted. The entire history of democracy proceeds on the presumption, right or wrong, that an electorate at any given time in the past must be treated as representing the entire population of that time unless there is a strong reason to make an exception in some particular matter.

When the representatives of the thirteen states of America signed the Declaration of Independence, the only people allowed to vote were a few white males. Should we then stop calling that document the *American* Declaration of Independence? No African-Americans had the right to vote when Abraham Lincoln got elected as the President of the US, so should the Emancipation Proclamation signed by Lincoln to liberate the African-Americans from slavery be repealed for being undemocratic? Today, universal adult suffrage means that all citizens 18 years old or more can vote, but at one time it used to mean that only citizens 21 years or older could vote, and this does not make us say that we did not have adult universal suffrage until the minimum age of voting was reduced to 18. Otherwise, if at some time in a remote future, the age of suffrage is reduced to 15, who would come to inform us in our graves that even we did not have universal adult suffrage?

Besides, in 1946, nobody in their right mind could have denied that the demand for Pakistan was much more popular among the lower segments of the society that were not eligible to vote. Even the critics of the Muslim League would have conceded this, while Jinnah is on record for saying, 'I had millions with me and especially [the] masses. The intelligentsia came last; the masses came first.'[1]

Therefore, the decision to partition India must be seen as having been taken by the Muslims of British India, and should be respected as their democratic right. It was their democratic right, because, *India had never been a federation until then.* This is the second important fact that the perpetrators of the conspiracy theory have been wanting us to overlook.

India at that time was a collection of several provinces and approximately five hundred states, each of which had been a

---

[1] 9 August 1947; Ahmad (ed.), *The Nation's Voice,* Vol.6, p.348

separate entity at the time of its surrender to the British and had been ruled by the British on terms and conditions that often varied from province to province, and from state to state. The British revealed their intention to create a federation in the Subcontinent only in the 1920s, and then the Hindu extremists led by Gandhi demanded that all areas conquered by the British at different times should be coerced into a single federation and handed over to the Congress. The Muslims proposed that the zones where the Muslims were in majority should be made a separate federation.

As such, the demand for Pakistan was not even a move to secede from an existing federation but a suggestion for bringing together some consenting provinces into a federation where no federation had ever existed before – not unlike how some provinces of North America had come together in 1867 to form the country we now call Canada. What could be wrong about such a demand, and if the creation of Pakistan was a British conspiracy then the creation of Canada was, like, what? A French conspiracy?

This might not have become so complicated had Gandhi and his associates been straightforward. Their claim over the provinces of Muslim majority was as false as the claim of Germany over Poland at that time.[1] But while the Germans had an army, Gandhi and his associates had none. Their trick was, in the words of Jinnah, 'to dominate and rule over the Mussalmans and other minority communities of India with the aid of British bayonets.'[2] Or, as the American pioneer of management sciences Mary Parker Follett had said about Gandhi:

Surely his method of non-co-operation was a use of power, the only power he and his followers had: the non-payment of taxes, the boycotting of English merchandise,

---

[1] This was elaborated by Jinnah on several occasions, including his presidential address at the Delhi session of the Muslim League session in April 1943, where he also quoted from *Indian Pageant* by Maj. F. Yeats-Brown; Yusufi (ed.), *op. cit.*, pp.1717-1718

[2] 18 August 194. Yusufi (ed.), *op. cit.*, p.2383

refusal of honours and titles, of civil and military posts, refusal to attend schools, etc. Gandhi made declaration of 'war to the end.' Well, war is war.[1]

What has been stated here should also be sufficient to establish that the full responsibility for the massacres and human misery that accompanied the so-called Partition of India rests with Gandhi and everybody else who opposed the creation of Pakistan (such persons included the last British Viceroy Lord Mountbatten and the British Prime Minister Attlee, who reiterated their preference for a united India even at the time of announcing the Partition on 3 June 1947).

5

Let's now get rid of a few minor theories that have been floated about the reason for the British departure from India.

Since the Congress had practically sided with the Axis Powers during the Second World War, its followers developed a cult of idealizing Hitler. The cult survived long after the Nazi leader had put a pistol in his mouth to end his misery and the world's. After independence, some of these brown Nazis began to think retrospectively (and wishfully) that the British left India due to the tough time the late Fuhrer and his friends had given them, never mind the eventual victory of the Allies against the Axis.

Other writers suggested that the departure of the British might have been partially or mainly due to the activities of a so-called Indian National Army – a group of Indian militants led by a former president of the Congress, who had helped the Nazis and

---

[1] 'Power' (1925) by Mary Parker Follett; Metcalf and Urwick (ed.), *Dynamic Administration: The Collected Papers of Mary Parker Follett*, p.81

the Japanese during the Second World War (more about this shady business in the last chapter of the book).

Others still give credit to an unspecified number of non-commissioned natives in the Royal Indian Navy, who had gone on strike for eight days in February 1946 because they wanted better conditions at work.

Of course, since the world had tolerated the most absurd idea that Gandhi had caused the British to leave India, other absurd thoughts were bound to follow in abundance. The authors of the propositions mentioned here forget the crucial and the most significant fact that the Congress joined the Constituent Assembly of India set up by the British in December 1946, i.e., *after these events*. It had then become a matter of obvious self-interest for the Congress that the British should stay.

This meant that the British rulers could now rely on the Congress to give them everything they needed in order to recover from any shocks that might have left them shaken but not stirred – no more nightmares about future mutinies, now that they were getting bed and breakfast from the Ma Baker of all seditionists itself.[1]

Having dispelled the fallacies, let's now proceed to understanding *How Jinnah Liberated India*.

---

[1] The allusion here is to the protagonist of the 1977 ballad by Boney M rather than the historical person (whose name is spelled Ma Barker and whose alleged role as the leader of her son's gang has been questioned by historians). There are a few other 'Easter eggs' of this kind in the book, and the readers are advised to look out for them.

2. Dr Jekyll and Mr Hyde

Originally the British had not set out with the intention of building an empire. The charter Queen Elizabeth I granted to the British East India Company in 1600 allowed monopoly over trade with India, but not a license to conquer territories. In the later modifications of the charter, the Company was permitted to hold some lands in India but only in order to secure its commercial interests. The unauthorized conquest of Bengal by Lord Robert Clive in 1757 scandalized many in London, and was questioned in the Parliament.

It was eventually realized that India was incapable of keeping itself free from foreign occupation, and if the British did not take it, some other foreign power would. Thereafter, the Company was permitted to take Indian states but was also required to look after the interests of the Indian people. The performance of the Company was scrutinized by the Parliament, usually every twentieth year at the time of renewing the charter.

These measures might not have been as effective as they were meant to be, but India was never without some sincere advocates in the British parliament. Successive generations of Indians would feel amazed, thrilled and inspired by the speeches delivered on their behalf in the British Parliament by Edmund Burke during the trial of Warren Hastings in 1794, or by Lord Macaulay in 1833:

> What is power worth if it is founded on vice, on ignorance, and on misery...? We are free, we are civilized, to little purpose, if we grudge to any portion of the human race an equal measure of freedom and civilization...
>
> The destinies of our Indian empire are covered with thick darkness. It is difficult to form any conjecture as to the fate reserved for a state which resembles no other in

history, and which forms by itself a separate class of political phenomena. The laws which regulate its growth and its decay are still unknown to us. It may be that the public mind of India may expand under our system till it has outgrown that system; that by good government we may educate our subjects into a capacity for better government; that, having become instructed in European knowledge, they may, in some future age, demand European institutions. Whether such a day will ever come I know not. But never will I attempt to avert or to retard it. Whenever it comes, it will be the proudest day in English history. To have found a great people sunk in the lowest depths of slavery and superstition, to have so ruled them as to have made them desirous and capable of all the privileges of citizens, would indeed be a title to glory all our own.[1]

Thus emerged the most curious and the most significant trait of the British society in its role as an imperial power. It was the conflict between two contradictory currents in the stream of its consciousness: consent and coercion.

The principle of consent, represented so well by the likes of Burke and Macaulay, embodied a genuine desire to see the day when India would become capable of independence. This current of thought could be attributed to the British nation itself ('our arts and our morals, our literature and our laws', as Macaulay mentioned proudly while elaborating this principle). Therefore by default it was symbolized by the British monarchs of the era and was epitomized by Queen Victoria ('a great and good Queen', as Jinnah was going to call her on the eve of independence[2]). In the known history of empires, this current of

---

[1] Macaulay, *Speeches* (Vol.1). pp.194-195
[2] Jinnah's toast to King George VI on 13 August 1947; Yusufi (ed.), *Speeches, Statements and Messages of the Quaid-e-Azam*, p.2607

thought might have been unique to the British ('a title to glory all our own', as Macaulay had described it).

The opposite idea of coercion expressed itself through actions that could delay the moment of India's independence as much as possible. This current of thought could be discerned in many of the powerful and ambitious leaders of Britain – the type that had thrived in almost every empire in the past.

The conflict that took place in the British conscience between the principle of consent and the practice of coercion was summarized by Jinnah when he said, 'there never was any question about the principle, but there remained always the question of how and when.'[1] A strange case of Dr Jekyll and Mr. Hyde? In the times to come, the first current of thought would become known as Commonwealth and the second, Imperialism.

Distinguishing between these two currents is extremely important if we want to make sense of history, because, as we will see in the next two chapters, almost all the pioneers of the Indian struggle for independence based their efforts on an understanding of this bipolar tendency of the British mind.

We fail to see this today because imaginary and real grievances against the British make us irrational. Muhammad Ali Jauhar, one of the pioneers of the Muslim League, would have liked us to know that this is mainly due to the basic human desire for revenge. Whenever a nation loses an empire, almost every nation that had formerly lived under that empire finds some grudge to hold up against the former master:

> Rightly or wrongly the Mussalman [Muslim] community ruled over India in one way or another from the eighth to the middle of the nineteenth century in some part of the country or another... A very important result of that with which we have to deal today is the feeling created by the record of Muslim rule for so long over so large a part of India. There is hardly a community that has not a real or

---

[1] *Ibid.*

an imaginary grievance against the old Muslim rulers...
Some have a grievance against [the Mussalman] because
he conquered Persia! Some have a grievance against him
because he conquered Byzantium, Syria and Egypt, and
did not lose Palestine in the Crusades! At any rate,
whosoever has ruled over India, whether it be the English
or the Mussalman, is bound in some way to suffer from
real or imaginary grievances of his old subjects.[1]

2

Today the Commonwealth is a voluntary association of 56
independent states best known for its social activities, but the
greatest minds who helped its evolution in its initial phases had
envisioned it to be much more. Such minds included Jinnah and
his colleagues – Muslims as well as non-Muslims. Therefore, in
this book, the word Commonwealth will not refer necessarily to
the association that exists today but also to the idea it once was,
and which might still evolve to become a bigger reality in the
future than what it is at present.

The crux of the idea was the principle of creative conflict –
diverse nations synthesizing their outputs to produce ideas and
institutions none of them could have produced alone. If wars
and conquests played a necessary role in the process, let us
outgrow the pain inflicted upon us and cherish what we now
have in our hands. Brave Indian princes like Sirajudaula,
Haider Ali and Sultan Tipu fought the British but once those
efforts failed and the British sovereignty over the Indian
Subcontinent was conceded, equally patriotic Indians like Sir

---

[1] Indian Round Table Conference (1931), *Proceedings of Sub-Committees,*
Volume 3, pp.160-161, 165

Syed Ahmad Khan and Dadabhai Naoroji cooperated with the British in order to achieve the same goal of national freedom through a different method. In the words of one of the closest friends of Jinnah and one of the greatest leaders of India, C. R. Das (Chittaranjan Das), 'through every success, through every failure, through every battle which was won, through every battle which was lost, the history of India was working out her destiny...'[1] In the words of Jinnah himself, 'I say this with no ill-will or offence. Some nations have killed millions of each other. That is not permanent. An enemy of today is a friend tomorrow. That is life. That is history.'[2]

In India, this ideal began to take a practical shape with the proclamation issued by Queen Victoria in 1858, reiterating the desire to establish equality between the Indian and the British citizens of the Empire – a principle that had long been conceded in theory. The Indian response to the Queen's proclamation was *The Causes of the Indian Revolt* by Syed Ahmed Khan (later Sir), emphasizing the need to include the natives in decision-making. This became the cornerstone of the British policy in the Subcontinent from that point onward.

Outside the Indian Subcontinent, the event that moved the British Empire in the direction of what we may call Commonwealth was the Confederation of Canada in 1867 – three provinces coming together to form a dominion virtually autonomous without breaking away from Great Britain.

The watershed year was 1886. Since representatives of British colonies were expected to gather in London the next year for celebrating the Jubilee of Queen Victoria, the Colonial Secretary invited them to a conference for discussing certain matters that required mutual consultation.

The Colonial Conference held in London in 1887 thus became the beginning of an evolutionary process that seems to have continued in stages of twenty years each. The stages are

---

[1] 14 October 1917; C. R. Das, *India for Indians,* p.67
[2] 24 April 1943; Yusufi (ed.), *op. cit.,* p.1711

listed in the following table and explained in the next section of this chapter.

STAGE	YEARS	OUTCOME
1	1887-1906	Decision to have regular conferences
2	1907-1926	Balfour Declaration of 1926
3	1927-1946	'Delhi Resolution' of Muslim League
4	1947-1966	Tashkent Agreement
5	1967-1986	SAARC
6	1987-2006	Afghanistan Compact
7	2007-2026	[Yet to be seen]

3

The first stage consisted of conferences held on an *ad hoc* basis – whenever the representatives of the colonies ended up in London due to any reason. By 1906, it had been decided that the conference should become a permanent institution, so that consultations may be held on a regular basis.

The conference held in 1907 marked the beginning of a new stage as the self-governing colonies of the Empire were given the name of dominions and the conference was renamed as Imperial Conference. This stage was completed in 1926, when dominions were recognized to be practically independent:

They are autonomous Communities within the British Empire, equal in status, in no way subordinate one to another in any aspect of their domestic or external affairs, though united by a common allegiance to the Crown, and freely associated as members of the British Commonwealth of Nations.[1]

The conference, now renamed the Commonwealth Conference, was thus faced with a most difficult question. All its dominions had a racial affinity with the parent nation of the Anglo-Saxon stock: Canada, Australia, New Zealand, Newfoundland, South Africa and the Irish Free State (later the Republic of Ireland). Could it be hoped that non-white nations, comprising the majority of the British Empire, would also join the Commonwealth? How?

The test case was India, and Gandhi soon replied in the negative. The Indian National Congress unleashed a massive and completely false propaganda equating dominion status and membership of the Commonwealth with political slavery. On 26 January 1931, the Congress adopted a resolution to the effect that 'India must sever the British connection and attain Purna Swaraj or complete independence.'[2] Thereafter, the day was celebrated every year as 'Independence Day' and the promise never to join the Commonwealth was repeated annually until 1947.

The way out of this deadlock was the demand for Pakistan (as already explained to some extent, with more details to follow throughout this book). A resolution adopted by the legislators of the All-India Muslim League in Delhi on 9 April 1946, which we may call the 'Delhi Resolution of the Muslim League' or the '1946 Delhi Resolution', laid down the basis on which India was

---

[1] Imperial Conference, *Summary of proceedings,* p.12
[2] Indian National Congress, *The Indian National Congress 1930-34; being the resolutions passed by the Congress, the All India Congress Committee and the Working Committee during the period,* p.1

going to obtain self-rule and join the Commonwealth: not as one dominion, but two.

A new stage started in 1947 when, contrary to the eighteen-year-long campaign by Gandhi and his associates against any part of the Subcontinent joining the Commonwealth, both India and Pakistan joined as independent dominions. Jinnah became the first non-white Governor-General appointed by the Crown. In his toast to King George VI, he said:

> Such voluntary and absolute transfer of power and rule by one nation over others is unknown in the whole history of the world. It is the translation and the realization of the great ideal of Commonwealth which now has been effected and hence both Pakistan and Hindustan have remained members of Commonwealth, which shows how truly we appreciate the high and noble ideal by which the Commonwealth has been and will be guided in the future.[1]

King George VI in his message to Jinnah and his people, said, 'In thus achieving your independence by agreement, you have set an example to all freedom-loving people throughout the world.'[2]

Having taken yet another U-turn, the Indian leadership had also decided to join the Commonwealth, but explicitly added its desire that Pakistan be coerced back into the Indian federation.[3] The second largest political party of India, the Hindu Mahasabha, had reiterated even more bluntly that 'there will never be peace unless the separated areas are brought back into the Indian Union and made its integral parts.'[4]

India had thus walked into the Commonwealth wearing the shoes of Imperialism, with the desire to coerce a fellow

---

[1] Jinnah's toast to King George VI on 13 August 1947; , *op. cit.,* pp.2607-2608
[2] Constituent Assembly of Pakistan, *Debates,* 14 August 1947, p.49
[3] Resolution adopted by the All-India Congress Committee on 15 June 1947; Mitra (ed.), *The Indian Annual Register Jan-Jun 1947,* p.123
[4] Resolution adopted by the All-India Committee of the Hindu Mahasabha on 8 June 1947; *ibid,* p.256

dominion into annexation. If 1947 marked the beginning of the stage where the ideal of Commonwealth was becoming a reality, then the stage could only be completed once India embraced the fact that the sovereignty of Pakistan was beneficial for the region. This was conceded by India in 1966, through the Tashkent Declaration.[1]

Great Britain was not involved in the creation of SAARC (South Asian Association for Regional Cooperation) in 1985-1986, yet the event should be considered the next milestone in the evolution of the Commonwealth for the following reasons.

Firstly, the formation of SAARC was the realization of a principle proposed by one of Britain's greatest thinkers, John Bright, who had been loved by the Indians as long as he lived. In 1858, he had predicted that the progress of the Subcontinent depended on its distribution into no less than five zones ('presidencies'), so that:

> ...if at any future period the sovereignty of England should be withdrawn, we should leave so many Presidencies built up and firmly compacted together, each able to support its own independence and its own Government; and we should be able to say we had not left the country a prey to that anarchy, and discord which I believe to be inevitable if we insist on holding those vast territories with the idea of building them up into one great empire.[2]

Secondly, all seven states that formed the SAARC were former colonies of the British Empire. They based their charter on 'respect for the principles of sovereign equality, territorial integrity, national independence, non-use of force and non-interference in the internal affairs of other States and peaceful

---

[1] The text of the declaration is available from https://peacemaker.un.org/india-pakistan-tashkent-declaration66 (retrieved August 2022)

[2] 24 June 1858; James E. Thorold Rogers (ed.), *Speeches on Questions of Public Policy by John Bright MP,* Vol.1, p.54

settlement of all disputes.'[1] Although these principles had been inherent to the religion and philosophy of some of the participating nations, the British had played a major role in showing the nations of South Asia how to apply these cherished principles in modern politics. These nations, having no racial affinity to the British, were now applying those principles for creating a little Commonwealth of their own – 'That there's some corner of a foreign field / That is for ever England.'[2]

Throughout their presence in the Subcontinent, the British had remained at loggerheads with Afghanistan, and the country had given them scary nightmares:

> When you're wounded and left on Afghanistan's plains,
> And the women come out to cut up what remains,
> Jest roll to your rifle and blow out your brains...[3]

Therefore, the Afghanistan Compact signed in London in 2006 could be seen as a turning point – 65 states and 15 international organizations hosted by Great Britain announcing their support for the people of Afghanistan in building 'a democratic, peaceful, pluralistic and prosperous state based on the principles of Islam'.[4] Even in the Commonwealth itself, a new stage had started to unfold by this time, as membership became available to states that had never been part of the British Empire, starting with Mozambique in 1995.

---

[1] The SAARC Charter, available from https://www.saarc-sec.org (retrieved August 2022)
[2] The lines are from the famous poem 'The Soldier'; Rupert Brooke, *1914 and other Poems,* p.15
[3] Lines are from the poem 'The Young British Soldier'; Rudyard Kipling, *Barrack-Room Ballads and other Verses,* p.56
[4] The Afghanistan Compact 2006, available from https://www.diplomatie.gouv.fr (retrieved August 2022)

4

At every stage of this evolution up until now, we witness a victory of the nobler current of the British thought, described here as 'Commonwealth'. It is always a victory over demons created by the other side of its own mind – the side that desires coercion and manifests itself as Imperialism.

Throughout the period covered by these seven stages, the coercive current of Imperialistic thought had been creating demons that threatened to halt this evolution.

For instance, the brutality of the colonialists in Africa presented an experience so different from the semi-benevolent rule of the British over the Subcontinent that Iqbal had to condemn the British conqueror of Sudan, Lord Kitchener, as a modern-day Pharaoh.[1]

Sometimes, the coercive streak of Imperialism could present itself through the same individual who was representing the nobler current of consent and Commonwealth in some other way. The declaration of 1926, recognizing the independence of dominions, was called the Balfour Declaration after Sir Arthur Balfour – the statesman who had in 1917 given his name to a declaration that paved the way for creating Israel against the consent of the inhabitants of the disputed territory.

Sir Winston Churchill helped save human civilization from annihilation at the hands of the Axis Powers during the Second World War, and sincerely desired that war, tyranny and poverty should be eradicated from the face of the earth permanently. But the solutions he presented for achieving these ends after WW2 were steeped in his Imperialistic outlook, and he proposed that (a) peace could only be ensured by developing more destructive weapons; (b) tyranny could only be defeated through a closer bonding between the white races of Europe and North-America,

---

[1] The passage appears in Iqbal's Persian epic poem, *Javid Nama* (1932). For a quick English abridgement, check Hina Tanvir, *Javidnama*, pp.23-24

34

excluding the coloured nations; and (c) poverty could be eradicated only through capitalism.[1]

The first of these ideas precipitated a race for armament that is now threatening the very existence of the planet. The second idea encouraged the Cold War and a cult of Super Powers. The third idea seems to have made us citizens of an artificial world in which everything that glitters is gold, and one can pursue private greed without worrying about the starving another.

Yet, the greatest demon unleashed by the Imperialistic current of British thought was the One India Theory, i.e. the idea that the Subcontinent was one country and one nation.

This was coercion, because neither the provinces and the states nor the nations inhabiting the region had ever agreed to it (as already mentioned). The theory caused perpetual strife between the Hindus and the Muslims during the British Rule and a horrible holocaust at the end of it, and has been continuing to hold back the progress of the South Asians nations even after the end of the British rule.

The theory was perpetuated because the best minds in Britain had always understood that the Subcontinent could never become a single country (as evident from the speech delivered by John Bright against this theory in 1858, quoted earlier). Knowing full well that the idea of a united India would keep the people of India fighting among themselves, the sinister side of British genius turned the age-old principle of 'divide and rule' on its head – *Unite and Rule!* In the words of Jinnah:

> The one thing which *keeps* the British in India is the false idea of a United India, as preached by Gandhi. A united India, I repeat, is a British creation – a myth, and a very dangerous myth, which will cause endless strife. As long as that strife exists, the British have an excuse

---

[1] 'The Sinews of Peace' speech (also called 'the Iron Curtain' speech) delivered by Churchill on 5 March 1946 is available from https://winstonchurchill.org (retrieved August 2022)

for remaining. For once in a way, 'divide and rule' does not apply.[1]

When the final decision to leave India was debated in the House of Lords in February 1947, one of the major arguments against leaving India was that British rule was necessary for the unity of India. 'The unity of India which the Government now seeks to disturb is, perhaps, the greatest blessing which British rule has brought,' said the Earl of Munster. 'To the world India is one country, and all her races, whatever their various religious beliefs, are Indians. When British rule ceases, without any agreement amongst the main Indian Parties, is all this unity to disintegrate…?'[2]

5

If the British conscience is capable of slaying the demons of its creation by its own sword, it should be enlisted by those who are fighting against the demons of British creation.

This principle formed an essential component of the strategy adopted by Jinnah and his school of thought in their struggle for the independence of India (as pointed out by King George VI in the message he sent them in the end: 'In thus achieving your independence by agreement, you have set an example to all freedom-loving people throughout the world.').

'We are not asking the British to quit India overnight,' Jinnah had said almost four years before independence. 'The British have helped to make this gigantic muddle, and they must stay and help to clear it up. But before they can do that, they will have to do a lot of hard thinking.' He went on to add:

---

[1] Quoted by Beverley Nichols in *Verdict on India,* p.193
[2] The House of Lords Debate on 25 February 1947, available from https://hansard.parliament.uk (retrieved August 2022)

It's a habit they don't find very congenial; they prefer to be comfortable, to wait and see, trusting that everything will come right in the end. However, when they do take the trouble to think, they think as clearly and creatively as any people in the world.[1]

This was also fair to the soul of Britain itself – why should the British people not get the opportunity to feel proud by participating to solve a problem created by their leaders? Why should Jane Eyre not be allowed to rescue Rochester after the madwoman in the attic has burnt down the house?

However, this could not be achieved by a mere appeal to the compassion of the British, nor by emotional blackmail. 'The heart of an eagle does not melt for a bird it is holding in its talon,'[2] Iqbal had said to those who might have been thinking that the British would leave the Subcontinent out of sheer pity.

A strategy was required, based on what Mary Parker Follett would have described as constructive conflict: bring the differences into the open, face the real issue, uncover the conflict, and unity will precipitate itself when a simultaneous revaluation of interests occurs on both sides.[3]

This is what the British writer Beverley Nichols experienced halfway through his interview with Jinnah in 1943, as he realized what was happening to him, or rather was *not* happening. Nichols was not losing his temper. This was remarkable because, as Nichols explained later:

Jinnah had been almost brutally critical of British policy... but his criticism had been clear and creative. It was not merely a medley of wild words, a hotchpotch of hatred and hallucination, in the Hindu manner. It was more like a

---

[1] Quoted by Nichols in *Verdict on India,* pp.191-192
[2] The verse appears in Poem 61 of Section 2 of the Persian book of Iqbal's poetry, *Zabur-i-Ajam* (1927). Translation is my own.
[3] 'Constructive Conflict' (1925) by Mary Parker Follett; Metcalf and Urwick (ed.), *Dynamic Administration: The Collected Papers of Mary Parker Follett,* pp.10-11

diagnosis. The difference between Jinnah and the typical Hindu politician was the difference between a surgeon and a witch doctor. Moreover, he was a surgeon you could trust, even though his verdict was harsh.

'The British must realize,' he had said to me before we tackled the problem of Pakistan, 'that they have not a friend in the country. Not a friend.'

A Hindu politician would have said that at the top of his voice, with delight. Jinnah said it quietly, with regret.[1]

Before we see how Jinnah enlisted the British conscience in his fight against the ugliest demon created by the British Imperialism, let us understand the tool he used. It was the All-India Muslim League, described by Jinnah as the 'national organization' of his people.

---

[1] Nichols, *Verdict on India,* pp.191-192

3. The soul of all human beings

While the ideal of Commonwealth was evolving through the seven stages mentioned in the previous chapter, the Muslim community of the Indian Subcontinent was going through seven stages of its own.

Just as British society was internally conflicted between the principles of consent and coercion, the Muslims had also come to the Subcontinent in two very different types of groups: conquerors and Sufis.

Dynasties of Arab, Turkish, Persian and Afghan origin had conquered parts of the Subcontinent at various times since 712 and almost the entire region by 1707, and had declined in power rapidly afterwards. The biggest of these empires was, of course, the famed Mughal Empire – best known to the world as the builder of the Taj Mahal.

The Sufis stayed away from the courts of these kings and emperors, and set up monasteries for teaching the masses how the unity of humankind could be discovered in the depths of one's soul. The immigrants and the native converts combined, and the Muslims of the Subcontinent eventually became the largest Muslim community of the world.

As power slipped away from the hands of this community, some of its visionaries and reformers saw it as a blessing in disguise. Not having a country to rule anymore, the community was now free to apply the Sufi methods of love to every walk of life, including those that had remained the exclusive domains of the kings and the emperors until then.

The exile of the last Mughal ruler in 1858 and the Proclamation of Queen Victoria soon afterwards prompted the great Muslim historian Syed Ahmad Khan (later known as Sir Syed) to start a movement for reorganizing the entire society on the principle of love as explained by the Sufis.

Speaking in 1863, he mentioned that there are countless levels of love according to the Sufi doctrine but five levels stand out. Firstly, there is love for those we know personally – friends, family, lovers or people we meet. Secondly, we can love the community to which we belong, even though we do not know all its members personally. Thirdly, there is love for humankind as a whole. Fourthly, love of Nature. Fifthly, love of the entire universe. Deploring the general apathy of the Muslims of his time, Syed asked them to start with the love of their community.[1]

It is futile to wonder why he did not base his reforms on love for all communities dwelling in the region or the Indian community in general. No such thing as an Indian community or an Indian nation existed at that time.

The customs of the Subcontinent, especially the religion of the Hindus (who formed a majority of three-fourth in the region), required that the followers of different religions should maintain distance from each other as a sign of mutual courtesy. A Hindu, especially one belonging to a higher caste, was forbidden to have food that had been touched by a Muslim, or to drink water from the same well as Muslims. Having Hindus work for the Hindu community and Muslims work for the Muslim community was the practical thing to do, and the efforts of Syed for organizing the Muslim community were therefore supported by many Hindu well-wishers as well.

Besides which, the Sufis had also held that there need not be any conflict between the love of one's own community and the love of humankind in general, or even the entire universe for that matter. These were just points on a continuum – stages in the same journey (not unlike what Macaulay had said in his famous speech of 1833, quoted in the previous chapter).

---

[1] Speech delivered by Syed Ahmad Khan (later Sir) in Calcutta on 16 October 1863. The original Persian text as well as an Urdu translation is included in the Urdu collection of Sir Syed's addresses edited by Panipati, *Khutbat-i-Sir Syed,* pp.39-56

In a story published in 1873, Syed symbolized the unity of humankind as a beautiful bride descending from the starry sky and saying, 'I am the soul of all human beings. I am the goodness that lasts forever. Whoever desires me should strive for the collective good of the entire humanity, and especially for the good of their own community.'[1]

2

But the most essential requirement of love in any form and at any level is to seek the consent of the beloved and to respect it unconditionally. Mutual consultation, therefore, was the operative principle of Syed's efforts from the very beginning.

The watershed year for this movement was 1886, just as it was for the idea of Commonwealth (as mentioned in the previous chapter). That year, when the Colonial Secretary in London was writing invitations to the chief executives of the colonies, Syed invited representatives from diverse segments of the Indian Muslim community to a conference in Aligarh, held on 27 December 1886.

The conference decided to form a permanent institution that became known as Mohammedan Educational Conference soon afterwards. Its aim was to meet every year so that Muslims from every part of the Subcontinent might consult each other over matters related to education and progress of the community.

The role of this conference in the history of the Indian Muslim community is comparable to that of the Colonial Conference in the life of the British Empire. The subsequent evolution of the Indian Muslim community has also comprised seven stages, often overlapping with the evolution of the

---

[1] Panipati (ed.), *Mazameen-i-Sir Syed,* Vol.5 (Urdu), p.261

Commonwealth described in the previous chapter. The stages are listed in the following table and explained in the next section of this chapter.

STAGE	YEARS	OUTCOME
1	1887-1906	Birth of All-India Muslim League
2	1907-1926	Election of 1926
3	1927-1946	'Delhi Resolution' of Muslim League
4	1947-1966	Tashkent Agreement
5	1967-1986	SAARC
6	1987-2006	Afghanistan Compact
7	2007-2026	[Yet to be seen]

3

The first stage started with the grim awareness that although the Muslims of India were called a community, they did not have any means for consulting each other. A definite goal was adopted, which was to enable the community to take unanimous decisions through mutual consultation. The goal was achieved in 1906, with the birth of the first country-wide political organization of the community, the All-India Muslim League.

The birth of the League was unlike any other political party of modern times anywhere in the world. A political party is usually founded by a particular school of thought due to its difference of opinion with the rest of the nation. The League, on the other hand, was formed after consulting every school of thought in the community – some five thousand Muslim individuals and organizations from across the British India – and with as much consensus as possible. The goal adopted twenty years earlier to enable the community to take its decisions collectively, was thus achieved.

Unlike any other political party, the League was a platform for any school of thought within the community to come forward and guide others with the agreement of the majority. The creed of the League was to seek good relations with the government and with other communities living in the country, and its definite goal was to secure for the Muslims the right to choose their own representatives, i.e. separate electorates. The goal was achieved in practical terms with the election of 1926. (Although the principle of separate electorates had also been applied in two previous elections, the turnout in those elections was very low).

The third stage started with the aim of removing certain anomalies in the constitution that to date had made the formation of Muslim-majority governments impossible, even in the provinces in which Muslims were a numerical majority. The process led to the idea of Pakistan, as first articulated by the philosopher-poet-politician Dr Sir Muhammad Iqbal in 1930 and officially adopted by the League in 1940. This goal was achieved when the elected legislators of the Muslim League adopted the Delhi Resolution in 1946.

From this point onwards, the evolution of this community is virtually the same as the evolution of the Commonwealth described in the previous chapter because, as we have seen there, the subsequent stages of both streams appear to be moderated by the Delhi Resolution adopted by the legislators of the Muslim League in 1946.

This should show us that there is a current of history with a will and a mind of its own, which seems intent upon creating a unity of sovereign states through common ideals and common institutions.

This is what Iqbal meant when he wrote, 'The life of modern political communities finds expression, to a great extent, in common institutions – Law and Government; and the various sociological circles [i.e. societies]... are continually expanding to touch one another.'[1]

He had also pointed out that the key for understanding this invisible current of history is the spiritual connection between the Muslim masses and the West: 'The most remarkable phenomenon of modern history... is the enormous rapidity with which the world of Islam is spiritually moving towards the West.'[2]

One example of this phenomenon is how the evolutionary processes of the Commonwealth and the Muslims of the Subcontinent have merged into one, as we have seen here. However, this is not the only example.

4

On 15 December 1947, the All-India Muslim League Council decided that there would be separate Muslim League organizations for Pakistan and the Indian Union (as India after partition was known until 1950), respectively called the All-Pakistan Muslim League and the Indian Union Muslim League.

By the mid-1950s, both organizations had lost their defining characteristic of a platform open to all schools of thought in the nation. In Pakistan, the League was stripped of power in 1953 and banned completely a few years later.

Even then, the League could be called the mother of the Pakistani parliament just as John Bright had called England 'the

---

[1] 'Political Thought in Islam' (1908) by Iqbal; Sherwani (ed.), *Speeches, Writings and Statements of Iqbal,* p.141
[2] Iqbal, *The Reconstruction of Religious Thought in Islam,* p.7

mother of parliaments'[1]. The League had practically served as the parliament of Muslim India even before independence, being a platform for every school of thought within the nation. Also, its demand for Pakistan was actually a demand for a separate constituent assembly, and that assembly became the parliament of Pakistan upon its creation.

Once we recognize the League as the mother of the Pakistani parliament, we can see that the evolution of parliament in Pakistan has been following exactly the same process that was followed by the parliament of England in its evolutionary phase.

In England there was a time when monarchs ruled by Divine Right and the parliament had very little power. Likewise, in Pakistan, every acclaimed school of thought had revolted openly either against the parliament or its mother, the League, within a few years of the creation of the country. In 1954, the usurpers of power even dissolved the parliament, and the highest court of the country ruled in their favour the next year by declaring that the parliament had never been sovereign. The next sixteen years in Pakistan thus became similar to those centuries in Britain when the rulers used to have the most power, and the parliament existed only in the name and by permission of the rulers.

In Britain the turning point came when Charles I dissolved one parliament in 1640, established a second in its place and then started a long-drawn conflict with that one too. The conflict led to two civil wars: a long and disastrous one in 1642-1643, and a shorter one in 1648-1649. The second of these civil wars led to the execution of Charles in 1649.

Similar things happened in Pakistan. In 1970, the feudalist-turned-politician Zulfikar Ali Bhutto came into conflict with two parliaments, respectively convened after the elections of 1970 and 1977. In the first instance, he declared that he would 'break the legs' of anybody who dared to attend a session of the parliament (Charles I could not have said it better). In the second

---

[1] Speech delivered in Birmingham on 18 January 1865; Rogers (ed.), *Speeches on Questions of Public Policy by John Bright* (Vol.2), p.112

instance, Bhutto convened the parliament even though the opposition had boycotted it. The two conflicts led to two civil wars: the more disastrous one in East Pakistan in 1971, and a lesser one in West Pakistan in March and April 1977 (usually downplayed by Pakistani historians). The second civil war led to the removal of Bhutto from power in 1977 and his execution two years later, just as the second civil war in England had led to the execution of Charles.

It is impossible to miss the striking similarities between the two men who got Charles and Bhutto executed: respectively, Oliver Cromwell and General Zia-ul-Haq. Both rose to power at the head of armies, both claimed to be Godly men and tried to introduce religious laws, and both were maligned after their death.

After Cromwell and Zia came the restorations, respectively, of the son of Charles I and the daughter of Zulfikar Ali Bhutto. Benazir Bhutto and the rulers who came after her up to 2018 can be treated collectively as the Pakistani equivalents of Charles II – gleefully asserting their superiority over the parliament and getting away with it because the people were reluctant to risk another civil war.

Next came James II in Britain (from 1685 to 1688), and Imran Khan in Pakistan (from 2018 to 2022). The similarities between the two are uncanny.

The supporters of James hailed him as an embodiment of liberalism and enlightenment, while the rest of the country resented him for his arrogance – and the same goes for Khan.

James dismissed the parliament almost as soon as he assumed power in 1685. Khan remained in conflict with the parliament throughout his short-lived rule, ran his government mostly through ordinances, and eventually dissolved the national assembly after the majority had moved a motion of no confidence against him.

James was ousted from power because the army and the parliament had both deserted him, and so was Khan.

For the rest of his life (most of which was spent in exile), James never conceded that his removal was legitimate and never gave up his dream of regaining power. His followers, called Jacobites (from Jacobus, the Latin version of 'James'), refused to accept the new monarchs. They fought battles against the army at home, staged rebellions overseas and joined separatist movements that had already existed in parts of the country. In Pakistan, some of these actions have already been taken by Khan and his followers within the few months that have elapsed since the end of Khan's rule.

In Britain, the parliament and the army offered the crown to a daughter of James, who was married to the king of Netherlands. They ascended the throne jointly as Mary II and William III while accepting the Bill of Rights, which required them and their successors to always respect the dictates of the Parliament. This is called the 'Glorious Revolution' because monarchy became constitutional and so it remains to this date.

In Pakistan too, Khan has been replaced by a coalition government. If they and other political parties existing in Pakistan become completely respectful to the parliament of their country, Pakistan could become a kind of constitutional monarchy much like Britain.

While the political dynasties of Pakistan might aspire for this, however, the people do not. Therefore the Pakistani people may come to understand that the only way forward is to restore the organization that created the country and was the mother of its parliament, the original Muslim League. But first they would need to understand how the League differed from every other political party in the world.

5

The League is dead? Long live the League. The immortality of the Muslim League was an article of political faith for Jinnah. 'Men may come and men may go, but the League will live forever,' he had prophesied.[1]

This is what we have seen here. The League has been presumably dead for almost seventy years now but its spirit still moves in a mysterious way, its wonders to perform.

The immortality of the League is the fundamental difference between this entity and every other political party of modern times. It shows us that the League was not created by human beings. It was a creation of God.

It was this same entity that Sir Syed had described as 'the soul of all human beings'. The Sufis had trained the masses for more than a thousand years to discover this entity in the depths of their souls. During those centuries this entity could not manifest itself in the external world because society had been dominated by absolute monarchy ('groaning under the most atrocious forms of despotism'[2], according to Iqbal).

As the absolute monarchy ended, the masses were free to discover in the external world the unity that they had already learned to discover in the depths of their souls. 'Why cannot you who, as a people, can well claim to be the first practical exponent of this superb conception of humanity, live and move and have your being as a single individual?' Iqbal asked them in 1930, while addressing them as president of the League.[3]

---

[1] Presidential address at the famous Lahore session of the All-India Muslim League on 22 March 1940; Yusufi (ed.), *Speeches, Statements and Messages of the Quaid-e-Azam*, p.1168

[2] 'Islam as a Moral and Political Ideal' (1909) by Iqbal; Sherwani (ed.), *op. cit.* p.115

[3] Presidential address delivered at the Allahabad session of the All-India Muslim League on 29 December 1930; *ibid,* p.29

The Indian Muslims were better equipped for this undertaking than any other Muslim community of the world. This was because, in the words of Iqbal, 'it is no exaggeration to say that India [i.e. the Indian Subcontinent] is perhaps the only country in the world where Islam, as a people-building force, has worked at its best.'[1]

The opportunity to carry out the experiment came under trying circumstances. The society was liberated from the absolute monarchy of the indigenous type only by a new foreign ruler that worked on its own routine of good cop, bad cop. The humane principle of consent and the coercive tendency of Imperialism were inflicted simultaneously by the British masters. 'Loss of political power is equally ruinous to nations' character,' Iqbal had noted in his private notebook in 1910:

> Ever since their political fall the Mussalmans of India have undergone a rapid ethical deterioration. Of all the Muslim communities of the world they are probably the meanest in point of character... but we are, I believe, still indispensable to the world as the only testimony to the absolute Unity of God – Our value among nations, then, is purely evidential.[2]

By these 'meanest in point of character', Iqbal was referring only to the middle classes and the elite, not the masses. The view was shared by many leaders of the League, especially Jinnah:

> Corruption is a curse in India and amongst Muslims, especially the so-called educated and intelligentsia. Unfortunately, it is this class that is selfish and morally and intellectually corrupt. No doubt this disease is common, but amongst this particular class of Muslims it is rampant.[3]

---

[1] *Ibid,* p.4
[2] Dr Javid Iqbal and Khurram Ali Shafique (ed.), *Stray Reflections,* p.27
[3] Ispahani (ed.), *M.A. Jinnah-Ispahani Correspondence 1936-1948,* p.69

Due to this selfishness, and moral and intellectual corruption, 'the so-called educated and intelligentsia' have neither been able to recognize what (or who) the League was, nor they have been able to see that its spirit has been practically shaping the destiny not only of their country but possibly the entire world.

The case of the masses, on the other hand, has always been different. It were the masses Iqbal had believed to be 'still indispensable to the world as the only testimony to the absolute Unity of God.' Consistent with this belief, he reminded his fellow leaders in 1932, 'The Muslim masses are not at all lacking in the spirit of self-sacrifice when the question of their ultimate destiny in this country is involved... The fault is ours, not theirs.'[1]

When the League adopted its demand of Pakistan in 1940, Jinnah said to the intelligentsia, 'I think that the masses are wide awake.'[2] He reiterated this observation after the achievement of Pakistan in 1947, as quoted earlier: 'The intelligentsia came last; the masses came first.'[3]

The League demanded of its leaders that they should not suggest goals for the people; instead, they should follow the goals adopted by the people. The leaders of the League believed that great ideas are created collectively by the entire society and not by a few individuals, as was stated by one of the pioneers of the League, Aga Khan III:

> The great lesson of modern history, to my mind, is that only those nations succeed and only those policies lead to national greatness, which are based not on ideas or ideals of a few leaders, however eminent, or of a few thinkers, but on the general consensus of views and opinions of the people.[4]

---

[1] Presidential address to the All-India Muslim Conference delivered on 21 March 1932; Sherwani (ed.), *op. cit.,* p.46

[2] 22 March 1940; Yusufi (ed.), *op. cit.,* p.1184

[3] 9 August 1947; Ahmad (ed.), *The Nation's Voice,* Vol.6, p.348

[4] Hafizur Rahman (ed.), *Report of the All-India Muslim Conference held at Delhi on 31st December 1928 and 1st January 1929;* p.20

Due to these reasons, the indestructible spirit of the League is not only carrying the evolutionary currents of its own society or that of the Commonwealth, but also that of its antagonist, the Indian National Congress. This is the final thing we need to understand before we can see how the League was used as a tool for liberating India.

4. Mistaken identities

In the first chapter of this book, we saw that the Indian National Congress was the handmaid of Gandhi in his struggle for delaying the independence of India from 1918 onwards. Before that year there used to be another party by the same name. In order to prevent confusion we might occasionally refer to these two parties by separate names: the original Congress and the Gandhian Congress.

The original Congress was founded by a group of enlightened Indians and their British friends in Bombay on 28 December 1885. It was the first political party of India and claimed to be among the pioneers of two fundamental concepts, India and its independence.

The British had been calling the entire Subcontinent a country by the name of India (and this usage is also followed in this book wherever applicable). However this did not really make India a country in the true political sense. Being a country in that sense would imply that all its diverse regions had agreed to share power among themselves. No such agreement had ever been made in the Subcontinent in five thousand years of its history. The task of making such an agreement to thereby create India in the political sense of a country, was the task that the Congress took upon itself.

The representatives of the Muslim community, such as Sir Syed and later the All-India Muslim League, completely agreed with this principle, although they differed about some of its practical implications, which will be discussed in the third section of this chapter. Hence, the Congress leader C. R. Das was not only speaking for his party but also for the Muslims of India when he said in 1917:

Chapter 4: Mistaken identities

Can you point your finger to any period of Indian history in which there was an united India? I have failed to discover it... Even in the time of Asoka there was not one whole united India; it was the domination of one country over the rest of India. The great Indian nationality of which I am speaking was not born then... and I say the purpose of Indian history is that throughout the ages, through every success, through every failure, through every battle which was won, through every battle which was lost, the history of India was working out her destiny and turning out the great Indian nation. Today we see the vision of that glory...

The history of India is working out – is bringing out gradually the soul of India – and the time will come... when India will stand before the whole world in all her glory of spirituality. The unity of the Hindus and the Mohammedans, and of all sects and creeds, will be bound together in one great cultural ideal and will influence the civilization of the world.[1]

Obviously, the independence of a country is an idea that cannot be conceived where there is no country in the first place, and hence the original Congress considered itself to be among those who were conceiving this idea from scratch, and not just striving to achieve it.

India had excellent armies when Alexander the Great invaded its north-western parts (now Pakistan). But the king of Taxila encouraged Alexander to attack the king of Jhelum, and another prince begged the foreign conqueror to march across the rest of the country. They were not traitors. The prince who wanted Alexander to march across India was Chandragupta Maurya, later the emperor of India and the grandfather of Asoka. They just did not have a reason to defend the whole of India, or to defend it for its own sake.

---

[1] 14 October 1917; C. R. Das, *India for Indians,* pp.67-68

Possibly the first occasion when the Indians expressed an almost unanimous desire to defend the whole of India against foreign aggression was when they stood up against a perceived threat of Russian invasion in 1885. The incident was mentioned, more than once, during the inaugural session of the Congress a few months later: 'Was not Russia sufficiently undeceived when, on the occasion of her threat, all the inhabitants of India, from the prince down to the peasant, vied with one another in placing the entire resources of their several States and their hard earned private fortunes, at the disposal of our Government?'[1]

2

The independence of India, therefore, was not just a matter of getting rid of the British. More essentially it required the Indians to evolve the type of consciousness necessary for conceiving and sustaining the idea of an independent country.

The work of the original Congress in this regard can be appreciated best in the light of a principle laid out by Iqbal (although he never joined the Congress, unlike his spiritual twin, Jinnah). Iqbal said that 'the perception of life as an organic unity is a slow achievement, and depends for its growth on a people's entry into the main current of world-events.'[2]

The watershed year for India's 'entry into the main current of world-events' was 1886, when a co-founder of the Congress became a candidate of the Liberal Party of the UK for election to the Parliament. He was the Parsi businessman and politician, Dadabhai Naoroji, often called the Grand Old Man of India. He had the full blessings of the Congress back home, and his British

---

[1] Indian National Congress, *Proceedings of the First Indian National Congress*, pp.103-104
[2] Iqbal, *The Reconstruction of Religious Thought in Islam,* p.133

supporters included the Lady with the Lamp, Florence Nightingale.

Although he did not win the election in 1886 (he succeeded in 1892), his nomination by one of the two major political parties of Britain marked the beginning of a new process.

It was the process through which the best minds of India and Britain could collaborate for evolving and fulfilling their noblest ideals. The independence of India, as one of those ideals, was to evolve gradually through this process rather than happen abruptly by revolution. This is what Naoroji implied when he said to his British voters during his election campaign:

> Standing as I do here, to represent the 250,000,000 of your fellow subjects in India, of course I know thoroughly well my duty; for if I am returned by you, my first duty will be to consult completely and fully the interest of my constituents. I do not want at present to plead the cause of India.[1]

The subsequent stages of the process are listed in the following table and explained in the next section of this chapter.

STAGE	YEARS	OUTCOME
1	1887-1906	Demand for self-rule in India
2	1907-1926	Election of 1926
3	1927-1946	'Delhi Resolution' of Muslim League
4	1947-1966	Tashkent Agreement
5	1967-1986	SAARC

---

[1] Chunilal Lallubhai Parekh (ed.), *Essays, Speeches, Addresses and Writings (On Indian Politics) of the Hon'ble Dadabhai Naoroji.*, pp.303-304

STAGE	YEARS	OUTCOME
6	1987-2006	Afghanistan Compact
7	2007-2026	[Yet to be seen]

3

The first stage, from 1887 to 1906, consisted of efforts for bringing India into the main current of world-events. It was completed when the Congress resolved that the long-term goal of India was to become a self-governing member of the British Empire, just like Canada, Australia and New Zealand. In other words, it meant the independence of India. Coincidentally, the session was presided over by Naoroji and turned out to be the first occasion when the newcomer Jinnah spoke in the Congress.

The second stage, from 1907 to 1926, consisted of steps that could gradually make India a self-governing dominion within the Commonwealth. Through its famous Lucknow Pact with the Muslim League in 1916, the Congress acknowledged that the most important steps were (a) the recognition of the Indian Muslims as a distinct political entity; and (b) the attainment of separate electorates for the Muslims. Therefore, this stage could be said to have been completed in 1926, when separate electorates became a practical reality.

The current of evolution represented by the original Congress had now become the same as that of the Muslim League, as the two currents had merged through the Lucknow Pact in 1916.

This process, however, did not include the ideals of Gandhi and his extremist followers who had taken over the Congress in 1918. This is where the distinction between the original Congress and the Gandhian Congress becomes crucial.

The demand for Pakistan put forward by the League during the next stage was an anathema to the Gandhian Congress but it was completely consistent with the principles established by the original Congress.

The fundamental principle on which the idea of Pakistan was based was that the Indian Muslims were a nation. This was not a new principle.

As Jinnah tried to explain in the Central Assembly of India in 1940, 'the Mussalmans always had at their back the basis—and it has never been different in the last twenty-five years—that they are a separate entity.' By the 'last twenty-five years', he meant since the birth of the Muslim League in 1906. A fellow member of the assembly suggested that 'at least that was not the view of Mr. Jinnah before 1920.' Jinnah disagreed and said, 'Since 1916, since the Lucknow Pact was passed on the fundamental principle of two separate entities.'[1]

Each of the five arguments upon which Jinnah built his case for Pakistan comprised of some principle upheld by the original Congress but discarded by its Gandhian reincarnation.[2]

The first argument of Jinnah was that India had never been a single country, and the myth of its unity was one of the two pillars of British imperialism.

We have already seen that the leaders of the original Congress understood that India had never been a single country in the political sense of the term. They might not have claimed outright that every effort to keep India united would perpetuate British rule, but this was implied in the 1858 speech of John Bright quoted in the previous chapter. It would suffice here to add that the foremost leaders of the original Congress regarded Bright as one of the sincerest friends of India. He was often quoted in the sessions of the Congress, including the session of

---

[1] Yusufi (ed.), *Speeches, Statements and Messages of the Quaid-e-Azam*, p.1268

[2] These arguments, summarized in this chapter, have been detailed with the help of quotes from the statements of Jinnah in *Jinnah: The Case for Pakistan* by Khurram Ali Shafique.

1906 where the goal of self-rule or independence for India was adopted for the first time.

The second argument of Jinnah was that the perpetuation of Western democracy in the Subcontinent was serving as the other pillar of British imperialism (along with the myth of India's unity). By Western democracy, Jinnah meant a party-system based on the principle of majority. This argument was consistent with what the original Congress had conceded through the Lucknow Pact.

The third argument of Jinnah in favour of Pakistan was that the idea demolished both pillars of British imperialism – the One-India fallacy and the party-based politics. Thus by demanding Pakistan, the Muslim League was seeking to liberate the entire Subcontinent.

This should have been obvious to anybody who remembered what had been said on the occasion of the Lucknow Pact by the foremost leader of the original Congress, Surendranath Banerjea:

> Today is a red-letter day in our history. Today, Hindus and Mohammedans and all ranks of the National party [i.e. Congress] are united on this platform, inspired by a common resolve and a common purpose. May the memory of this day be embalmed in the recollections of posterity by the inauguration of a new campaign for the attainment of self-government.[1]

The League had continued to follow the 'new campaign' launched on that day, and the demand for Pakistan was the only way to take that campaign forward beyond 1926.

The Gandhian Congress, on the other hand, strove to sabotage that campaign from the very beginning. This much had been pointed out by Banerjea himself in 1918, as we have seen in the first chapter ('the extremists are playing into the hands of Lord

---

[1] Indian National Congress, *Report of the Thirty-first Indian National Congress held at Lucknow on the 26th, 28th, 29th and 30th December 1916*, p.76

Sydenham and his party'[1]). This accusation levelled against the Gandhian Congress by the original party members comprised the fourth argument of Jinnah in his case for Pakistan. As already mentioned, Jinnah maintained that the Gandhian Congress and its allies wanted to keep the British in India, and their claim that they were fighting for independence was false.

The fifth argument of Jinnah in his case for Pakistan was that the most important outcome of any political activity should be the eradication of poverty and the uplift of the masses (freedom from 'want and fear'[2], as he described it). This was the real ideal of the original Congress.

The founding fathers of that organization were among the earliest generation of Indians to receive modern education, and they believed that the price of that education had been paid by the sweat and toil of the masses. 'I had been educated at the expense of the poor, to whom I myself belonged,' Dadabhai Naoroji had said while reminiscing his schooldays. 'The thought developed itself in my mind that, as my education and all the benefits arising therefrom came from the people, I must return to them the best I had in me. I must devote myself to the service of the people.'[3]

As we will see now, Gandhi and his school of thought did not want this to happen, as they were perpetuating a new form of caste system.

---

[1] Presidential address delivered by Banerjea on 1 November 1918; All-India Conference of the Moderate Party, *Report of the Proceedings of the First Session,* p.41
[2] 25 August 1947; Yusufi, *op. cit.* p.2615
[3] R. P. Masani, *Dadabhai Naoroji – The Grand Old Man of India,* p.35

4

The original Congress was known to have two factions: the moderates and the extremists.

The moderate group guided the Congress until 1918, when the extremists gained majority under the leadership of Gandhi. The surviving founders and their moderate followers left the Congress to form a new party under the guidance of Banerjea, who said, 'We could not but secede; for the differences between those who had captured the machinery of the Congress – call them Extremists for want of a better name – and ourselves were fundamental...'[1]

The new Congress sometimes pretended that it was the same organization that was founded in 1885, and sometimes admitted more honestly that it was not: 'The Congress, as at present constituted, is the creation of Mahatma Gandhi.'[2]

One of the brightest stars of the Gandhian Congress was Maulana Muhammad Ali Jauhar, a founding member of the Muslim League, who joined the Congress in 1919 and presided over it in 1923. It was primarily his influence that brought the Muslim masses to the folds of the Congress for a few years in the early 1920s (the only time when the Congress had a significant number of Muslims on its side).

By 1930, Jauhar had left the companionship of Gandhi and to him we owe the best insight into what Gandhi was all about. Jauhar said a few days before his death in January 1931:

---

[1] Presidential address delivered by Banerjea on 1 November 1918; All-India Conference of the Moderate Party, *op. cit.,* p.37

[2] Welcome address delivered on 10 March 1939 by Seth Govind Das, chairman of the reception committee at the annual session of the Congress held at Tripuri in 1939; Indian National Congress, *Report of the 52nd Indian National Congress Tripuri (Dt. Jubbulpore), Mahakoshal, 1939*, p.57.

The passage was also quoted by Jinnah in his presidential address to the Delhi session of the League in 1943; Yusufi, *op. cit.* p.1704

...for the first time in the history of India we intend to introduce into India majority rule, and those who have been usurping the control of the destinies of those called Hindus for so many thousands of years do not want that there should be any majority – Indian or Hindu – except that which they can control precisely as they have controlled the Hindus for thousands of years. Let me add that there is one important difference... The small monopolistic caste that desires to remain in control of the destinies of the Hindu community – and that being the majority community, of the Indian nation as a whole through it – is the caste not so much of [the Brahmin], but of the *banya* [merchant]... To my mind, most of the agitation to-day [i.e. the civil disobedience movement led by Gandhi in 1930-1931] is being financed, and partly for selfish reasons, by the *banyas* of Bombay and Gujrat... it is not the fight for India's freedom in its larger sense.[1]

This new caste system is not to be confused with the old one (forget the Brahmins, Kshatriyas, Vaishyas and the Shudras). The new caste system might be creating new castes that are yet to be recognized, but its method can be discerned in the fundamental differences between the original Congress and the Gandhian doppelganger.

Those differences include (a) the dictatorship of Gandhi; (b) a false narrative about 1857; (c) equating the Commonwealth with imperialism; (d) inviting foreign invasions on India; and (e) politics of violence.

Through these differences, we can see how a fake democracy is being created by reusing the techniques of the old caste system – degrade the people; take away their history; create an atmosphere of hostility, resentment and suspicion; and convince

---

[1] Indian Round Table Conference (1931), *Proceedings of Sub-Committees, Volume 3, p.162

the people that they are evil and inferior. We will now review this in a little more detail.

1. The dictatorship of Gandhi. Gandhi never stood for election, and yet the entire Hindu society and its elected representatives were told to start and stop countrywide movements of civil disobedience at his call. This was justified by telling the people that Gandhi was spiritually superior to them:

> Our Congress organization can be compared with the Fascist Party of Italy, the Nazi Party of Germany and the Communist Party of Russia, although they have embraced violence and we are wedded to the creed of non-violence... Mahatma Gandhi occupies the same position among Congressmen as that held by Mussolini among Fascists, Hitler among Nazis and Stalin among Communists.[1]

The Gandhian Congress was not wedded to the creed of non-violence as we are going to see presently, so the only real difference between the European dictators and Gandhi seems to be that the former were using modern ideologies for stamping their authority over the masses, while the latter was achieving that result by making the people believe that they were evil and inferior.

The first time Gandhi started a countrywide campaign in India in 1920, he said that God had told him India would be free within a year. When that did not happen, he said that God had informed him the people of India proved themselves unworthy of freedom. So, if Gandhi's prophecies failed, the fault was not his but that of the people!

This was a denial and a reversal of the basic premise of democracy, i.e. the general will cannot be wrong. But not only did the new caste system deny the general will, it also attempted

---

[1] *Op. cit.* welcome address delivered on 10 March at the Tripuri session of the Congress in 1939; Indian National Congress, *op. cit.,* p.57

to erase the people's history, without which they cannot recognize the general will in the first place. One example is how it presently prevents Indian Muslims from owning their recent history and even branding them traitors, as we saw in the first chapter. Further examples can be seen as we continue our review below.

2. A false narrative about 1857. By retrospectively calling the uprising of 1857 'the First Indian War of Independence', the Gandhian Congress has practically taken away from the people of the Subcontinent their history. In 1857, the Mutiny was understood as being an attempted genocide of the entire Christian population of the Subcontinent. With the exception of some extremists, every school of thought in India kept condemning it right up until the rise of the Gandhian Congress.

By relabelling that event as an 'Indian' war of 'independence', the Gandhian Congress not only erased sixty years of collective memory, it also denied the original Congress the credit for pioneering the concept of India and the idea of its independence. The pioneers of the original Congress were branded as traitors by default, since they had represented the Indians who helped the British stop the madness of 1857 (as was announced in the very first session of the Congress: 'Have we ever as a nation tried to oust the established Government in this country? Have we not crushed those deluded people, who under an erroneous conception supposed that their religion was intentionally attacked by the introduction of greased cartridges?'[1]).

3. Equating the Commonwealth with imperialism. Just as Nawab Sirajidaula and Sultan Tipu were honoured in India as rulers of a bygone era, Queen Victoria and her successors were loved and respected as rulers of the new era. Generations of Indians looked

---

[1] Speech by Rao Saheb Singarajee Venkata Subbarayudu Pantulu Garu (Masulipatam); Indian National Congress, *Proceedings of the First Indian National Congress*, p.139

forwards to the day when the Empire would give way to the Commonwealth. This experience has also been erased from the collective conscience due to the ambivalent attitude adopted by the Gandhian Congress and its successor, modern India, towards the idea of the Commonwealth.

4. Inviting foreign invasions on India. Part of the experience thus lost is the feeling of ownership that the people of India developed for their land, when they stood up to defend the whole Subcontinent against foreign aggression in 1885 (even if they did so for an existing government of foreigners, as mentioned earlier).

By negating this evolution, Gandhi was back in the mental atmosphere of the days when the great Chandragupta Maurya had begged a foreign conqueror to march through India. During the very first countrywide campaign of civil disobedience (1920-1922), Gandhi said that if Afghanistan should invade India he would tell Indians not to assist the Government in defending their country.[1] How Gandhi and his disciples overtly or covertly tempted the Nazis and the Japanese to conquer India during the Second World War will be seen in the next chapter.

Such ambivalence about the country's borders has remained the hallmark of modern India, the successor of the Gandhian Congress – the adoption of a national anthem that treats a province of another sovereign country as part of India; annexation of Kashmir against the will of its inhabitants; the invasion of East Pakistan for creating a country for which the people of that area had not voted; and so on.

---

[1] Statement made by Gandhi in a conference at Allahabad in May 1921 and quoted in *Histories of the Non-Co-operation and Khilafat Movements* by P. C. Bamford, p.29.

Gandhi expressed the same views in an article he published on 4 May 1921: 'I would, in a sense, certainly assist the Amir of Afghanistan if he waged war against the British Government. That is to say, I would openly tell my countrymen that it would be a crime to help a Government which had lost the confidence of the nation to remain in power.' Gandhi, *The Collected Works of Mahatma Gandhi*, Vol. 23, p.110

Thus Indians are not supposed to defend India as a country established by law, or to defend boundaries recognized internationally. They are supposed to defend territories, or not defend them, according to the whimsical desires of the narcissistic and megalomaniac owners of their destinies – Gandhi, the Nehru dynasty, Narindra Modi and whoever else.

5. Politics of violence. The international media was enamoured by Gandhi because Gandhi preached non-violence (and Donald Trump said to his supporters: 'peacefully and patriotically make your voices heard' at the Capitol building). The non-violence of Gandhi's teachings was strictly an export item, not for domestic consumption.

The Congress activists who carried out Gandhi's campaigns were notorious for coercing anybody who disagreed. This caused much bloodshed during all of the countrywide campaigns of Gandhi. One of the worst incidents was a communal riot in Cawnpore in 1931. Hundreds of Muslims were butchered, thousands were displaced, and the Congress acknowledged that it had all started due to the coercive methods of its activists.[1] Gandhi's own attitude towards such incidents of violence was always along the lines of smoke but don't inhale. One of his typical statements was, 'If non-violence has to fight the people's violence in addition to the violence of the Government it must still perform its arduous task at any cost. I see no escape from it.'[2] So, the Congress had new founding fathers now, and they wanted the purge.

Other parties joined the campaigns of Gandhi without even paying any lip-service to non-violence. These included Hindu

---

[1] This was freely admitted by many Congress leaders at that time but the most comprehensive statement from their side is the document popularly called 'The Cawnpore Committee Report' (referenced in the present book as Indian National Congress, *A History of the Hindu-Muslim Problem in India*). The section 'Coercion in the Hartal' appears in that document on pp.215-220
[2] Interview to Free Press of India, 17 April 1930; Gandhi, *The Collected Works,* Vol.49, p.123

revivalists who believed in the supremacy of the Aryan race, to which the high caste Hindus supposedly belonged; and they wanted to get rid of alien religions, especially Islam and Christianity. One revivalist organization, the Hindu Mahasabha (an indirect or direct predecessor of today's Bharatya Janta Party), visibly influenced the policies of Gandhi and his Congress after 1926. Its media openly interpreted Gandhi's rhetoric of non-violence as nothing more than a camouflage.[1] The followers of these organizations believed that Gandhi would help them fulfil their anti-Muslim and anti-Christian agendas in the end, and the results of Gandhi's campaigns never failed to disappoint them (they were, however, disappointed when Pakistan came into existence contrary to the expectations that Gandhi had raised in their hearts, and so they shot him till he was dead – oh, those Indians).

5

It was unfortunate that Hindu society was swept so completely by totalitarian leaders after 1926, but the same was happening to Germany, Italy, Japan and Russia around the same time.

And yet it seems to be a remarkable sign of our times that the remedies through which a society may overcome its own evils are usually found in the repertoire of the society itself. 'The spirit of Ancient India aimed at the discovery of God and found Him,' Iqbal wrote in 1925, and went on to suggest:

---

[1] For instance, the leading Mahasabha leader Lala Lajpat Rai wrote stated in an article in 1924 that 'it was an open secret' that a fast recently undertaken by Gandhi was intended by the latter as 'penance' for having cooperated with the Muslims earlier; Vijaya Chandra Joshi, *Lala Lajpat Rai: Writings and Speeches,* Vol.2, p.174

Fortified by this valuable possession, Modern India ought to focus on the discovery of man as a personality—as an independent 'whole' in an all-embracing synthesis of life—if she wants to secure a permanent foundation for her New Nationalism.[1]

By that time, the founding fathers of the original Congress had passed away. Their moderate followers were about to start following the line of the extremists, one way or another. Also dead was C. R. Das, arguably the greatest Hindu thinker of modern times, who can be credited with revealing the inner synthesis of life that Iqbal was suggesting here.

Das hailed from Bengal and started his career a little before Jinnah, who later became one of his closest friends. Das was a barrister, poet, philosopher and political leader. He was popularly called 'Deshbandhu', or the Patriot. He stayed with the Congress even after its takeover by Gandhi, and participated wholeheartedly in the campaign of 1920-1922 (Jauhar later said that he had persuaded Das to join Gandhi).

When the campaign failed, Das was quick to see the mistake. He suggested an alternative strategy for liberating India in his presidential address to the Congress in December 1922, and called it 'freedom through disobedience'.

Iqbal wrote that the political programme of Das embodied the same spiritual principle that Iqbal had presented a few years earlier in his own work.[2]

Significantly, Iqbal had claimed his principle to be derived from the Quran but also consistent with the teachings of Krishna as contained in Bhagavad Gita (and hence a Sikh politician friend of Iqbal was attempting an interpretation of Iqbal's work in the light of Gita). By analogy, the message of Das could be seen as derived from the Gita but also consistent with the Quran.

---

[1] A short note written by Iqbal on 5 December 1925 and published in January 1926 as 'The Inner Synthesis of Life'; Razzaqi (ed.), *Discourses of Iqbal*, p.267

[2] Urdu letter written by Iqbal to Abdul Majid Daryabadi on 6 January 1923; Dr S. M. H Burney, *Kuliyat Makateeb-e-Iqbal*, Vol.2, p.418

In his address, Das had quoted passionately from *The New State* (1918) by Mary Parker Follett and had said, 'There is thus a great deal of correspondence between this view of life and the view which I have been endeavouring to place before my countrymen for the last fifteen years.'[1]

Follett was an American, but the distinguished British politician-philosopher Viscount Haldane was recommending her ideas to his fellow Britons. Three decades later, the Japanese would use the same ideas for rebooting their economy after Hiroshima and Nagasaki.

Could it be more interfaith and cosmopolitan? A manifesto independently conceived by a Muslim, a Hindu and a Christian – respectively from the Quran, the Gita and the Bible – later to be picked up also by Japan. If the biggest empire of history had to go down, at least it deserved to be hit with a weapon of such magnitude and this much grace. It might not so much hurt then.

Das believed that humanity was evolving collectively and each nation represented a particular stream in that process. This was because 'the outer Lila of God reveals itself in history'.[2] This was not very difference from what Iqbal described as 'the Quranic view of the *"alternation of day and night"* as a symbol of the Ultimate Reality which *"appears in a fresh glory every moment"*[3]. Follett had also observed that 'Man and God are correlates of that mighty movement which is Humanity self-creating.'[4]

This is why parallel currents of evolution have been presented in this book, each representing a nation, all currents merging with one another through mutual consent, consultation and agreement (and not because the Man in the Moon had spoken to Gandhi). Identifying such currents was very important according

---

[1] C. R. Das, *Freedom Through Disobedience,* p.45
[2] *Ibid.*
[3] Iqbal, *The Reconstruction of Religious Thought in Islam,* p.135. The verses of the Quran quoted here are 2:164 and 55:29.
[4] Mary Parker Follett, *The New State,* p.103

to Das, because he understood that goals could be achieved only if we have identified the stream of our nation correctly:

> I contend that each nationality constitutes a particular stream of the great unity, but no nation can fulfil itself until it becomes itself and at the same time realises its identity with Humanity. The whole problem of nationalism is therefore to find that stream and to face the destiny. If you find the current and establish a continuity with the past, then the process of self-expression has begun, and nothing can stop the growth of nationality.[1]

Subject to this process of evolution, the strategy devised by Das can be said to have consisted of five action points (disregarding some technical details):

1. *Give complete reassurance to the religious minorities* that the independence of the country would also mean independence for them.

2. *Contest the election on a single-point agenda,* which should be independence. Every other detail, such as the system of government and the type of constitution should be left to be decided after independence has been achieved.

3. *Sweep the polls.* It was absolutely necessary that a single organization should win an overwhelming majority in the assembly, or almost all the seats, so that it could become the sole representative of the nation. This organization could not be a political party. It had to be what Follett was proposing by the name of 'group organization' and what Jinnah would later describe as 'national organization'. The difference between this type of organization and a political party has already been seen in the previous chapter, where we also saw that the All-India Muslim League happened to be the only

---

[1] Das, *Freedom Through Disobedience,* p.20

practical example of such an organization having existed. Indeed, the Congress came close to becoming a national organization when it incorporated the point of view of the Muslim League through the Lucknow Pact in 1916, but it wandered off in the direction of becoming a totalitarian party under the dictatorship of Gandhi only two years later. It would have become a national organisation, had it followed the strategy of Das.

4. *Do not cooperate with the assembly* after winning the majority of seats in it, or possibly all the seats. This would be the only way of sending across the message to the British *people* that the Indians wanted independence. The campaign of Gandhi had failed to convey this message effectively because while Gandhi agitated in the streets, general elections had been held and Indians who did not agree with Gandhi had got themselves elected. Why would an average citizen in Britain believe that the Indians did not want British rule when representatives elected by the Indians were sitting in the assemblies set up by the British?

5. *The result* would be the independence of India. This would happen because the people of Britain had a desire to lead India to its goal of becoming a self-governing independent state, and it was only a few politicians who were delaying it by misleading the British public. This is what the leaders of the original Congress had believed. If all of them had been wrong about this most fundamental assumption, what basis was there for an Indian struggle for independence in the first place?

Gandhi and his Congress rejected the proposal, but Das went ahead to try and implement it in any case, starting in 1923. His foremost ally in the assembly was, of course, his friend Jinnah.

Unfortunately, Das died on 16 June 1925. The veteran Banerjea also passed away on 6 August the same year.

Chapter 4: Mistaken identities

Through an irony of history, Jinnah was thus left as the only prominent leader of the original Congress still to be willing to tread the path laid out by the pioneers of that organization. He had resigned from the Congress, however, in 1920. Now he was only the president of the Muslim League.

Knowingly or unknowingly, the League ended up implementing the strategy of Das in the 1940s, as we are going to see in the next chapter. Hence, although it alone was responsible for getting independence for India, credit also belonged to the long-dead leaders of the original Congress. Those departed souls were also vindicated through the actions of the League and its 'great leader', Jinnah. Thus it remains possible for present-India to align itself with the vision of the original Congress should it choose to do so.

Paying his tributes to Das and Banerjea in the Central Legislative Assembly in 1925, shortly after their deaths, Jinnah said:

> Sir, I might say that I learnt my first lessons in politics at the feet of Sir Surendranath Banerjea. I was associated with him as one of his followers and I looked up to him as a leader. He commanded the utmost respect of a large body of people in this country and of my humble self. Sir, as far as Mr. Das is concerned, he was [a] personal friend of mine. I have enjoyed his hospitality, and he was one with whom I worked for many years.
>
> I feel that in the loss of these two great men, Bengal, nay India, has suffered an irreparable loss. And on this occasion I should like to say this, that these were leaders in this country for whom the Mohammedans had the greatest respect, and they commanded the confidence of the Mussalmans as much as any Mussalman leader.

Sir, the only lesson I feel that we might draw from the careers of these two great men is this that in unity lies salvation...[1]

---

[1] Syed Sharifuddin Pirzada (ed.), *The Collected Works of Quaid-e-Azam Mohammad Ali Jinnah,* Volume 2, p.386

5. How India was liberated

On 1 September 1939, the forces of Nazi Germany invaded Poland as ordered by their Fuhrer, Adolf Hitler. Two days later, the King-Emperor George VI informed his subjects through a now famous radio broadcast: 'For the second time in the lives of most of us, we are at war.'[1]

The Second World War, or WW2, had started. India's entry into the war was declared by Viceroy Lord Linlithgow. A few days later, he read out the king's message to the Indians in the Central Legislative Assembly at Delhi:

> I am confident that in the struggle upon which I and my peoples have now entered, we can count on sympathy and support from every quarter of the Indian Continent in the face of the common danger. Britain is fighting for no selfish ends but for the maintenance of a principle vital to the future of mankind—the principle that the relations between civilized States must be regulated, not by force, but by reason and law, so that men may live free from the terror of War, to pursue the happiness and the wellbeing which should be the destiny of mankind.[2]

In many ways, this was a repeat of 1885. At that time, there was a perceived threat of Russian invasion and the Indians had responded by standing up to defend the whole of their country,

---

[1] The broadcast was made at 9.00 pm on 8 May 1945 in UK. The speech has been the subject of the award-winning movie *The King's Speech* (2010). Original recording and a transcript is available at https://www.royal.uk (retrieved August 2022)
[2] Waheed Ahmad, *The Nation's Voice,* Vol.1, p.557

even though the country was under British rule. If that was the first indication that the Indians had developed a notion of independence, the response to the threat posed by WW2 was going to determine how much they had evolved during the past fifty-four years – or if they had failed to evolve.

The Viceroy met Gandhi, Jinnah and the representative of the native princes in order to obtain the support of their respective parties for the war efforts. The Congress refused after creating a little bit of drama which will be discussed in the next section. The native princes gave their support.

The League asked for a few reassurances, most importantly that no future constitution would be imposed on India without the consent of the minorities. The reply of the Viceroy did not sound quite reassuring, and so the League went ahead to prepare a consolidated statement.

The statement came out as the Lahore Resolution, later called the Pakistan Resolution, adopted in the annual session held in Lahore during the Easter holidays, 22 to 24 March 1940. Declaring the existing constitution to be unworkable, two fundamental principles were established for the future: (a) more than one independent states in the Subcontinent according to the wishes of the people; and (b) all rights of the religious minorities to be determined in consultation with them.

As already mentioned, the idea came to be known as Pakistan or the partition of India, and was compatible with the principles previously agreed between the Indian Muslims, the original Congress and the British.

If the British agreed to the demand for Pakistan, the League could wait for its realization until the end of the war, and would participate in the war efforts. Otherwise, it would refrain from actively participating in those efforts but it was not going to discourage the common Muslims from helping the British. It did not want the Nazis to win the war.

2

The position of Gandhi and his Congress became increasingly incomprehensible as the war progressed, until it became impossible to assign any meaning to it except one.

Under the India Act 1935, provincial governments were elected by the people (including a separate electorate for Muslims). Religious minorities were guaranteed safeguards, including a share in the government. In the election held in 1937, the Congress emerged as the biggest party but received very few votes from Muslims as they preferred other parties, in particular the Muslim League.

The central administration did not consist of elected representatives, and was under British control. It was represented in the provinces by governors, whose special powers included intervention if the safeguards of any minority were violated.

The Congress announced that it was joining the assemblies in order to make them unworkable through 'non-cooperation' and thus force the British to leave India (an idea originally presented by C. R. Das, but in a different spirit). They sought a promise from the governors to stop using their special powers, or the Congress would not accept provincial ministries.

Once this was promised by the government, the Congress asked Muslims elected on the tickets of other parties, including the League, to become turncoats and join the Congress. Otherwise they would not get what the constitution provided for them (since the special powers no longer protected them). The League had no reason to exist, according to the Congress president Jawaharlal Nehru: 'We have too long thought in terms of pacts and compromises between communal leaders and neglected the people behind them. That is a discredited policy and I trust that we shall not revert to it.'[1]

---

[1] Mitra (ed.), *The Indian Annual Register Jan-Jun 1937,* p.208

The Congress also demanded 'a Constituent Assembly, elected by adult franchise, to determine the Constitution of the country.'[1] Practically, it would mean a constitution dictated by the Congress but such a constitution would not be acceptable to almost half of India.

During the drafting of the existing constitution, practically all minorities except the Sikhs had denounced the Congress and had submitted a joint proposal (the 'Minorities Pact') which stood against everything that the Gandhian Congress believed in. In addition, there were approximately 500 native states ruled by princes through treaties with the British Crown, and the Congress had been usually hostile towards them.

Who would ensure that a constitution dictated by the Congress gets implemented against the wishes of almost half of the country? Only the British could, if they coerced the minorities on behalf of the Congress.

WW2 was treated by the Congress as a golden opportunity for pressuring the British to do this. Hence, when the Viceroy asked Gandhi to get him the support of the Congress, the Congress repeated its twin demands of immediate declaration of India's independence, and a constituent assembly. At the same time, it resigned from provincial governments (the trick that had worked in 1937 to make the British give up their special powers to safeguard the minorities). The trick didn't work this time.

After the League presented its demand for Pakistan, the Congress pressured the British to refuse it. The Viceroy promised a constituent assembly on 8 August 1940, with two caveats: (a) the assembly would be not be set up not immediately, but after the war was over; and (b) the minorities would not be coerced into accepting a constitution they did not want (since the League had specifically asked for this assurance). During the war, Indian representatives could join the Executive

---

[1] Resolution 6 of Congress Working Committee, February-March 1937; *The Indian National Congress 1930-34: being the resolutions passed by the Congress, the All India Congress Committee and the Working Committee*, p.42

Council of the Viceroy, i.e. the central administration, which had been exclusively under the British until then.

The Congress rejected this offer, because of the assurances to the minorities. Gandhi punished the British by launching a small-scale propaganda campaign against the war efforts of the British (he called it 'individual satyagraha'). Reminded by the Viceroy that this was contrary to the claims of the Congress that its policy was not to embarrass the British war efforts, the Mahatma replied that 'the Congress does still want to refrain from embarrassing the British government. But it is impossible for the Congress to make of the policy a fetish...'[1]

On 15 February 1942, Singapore fell to the Japanese. About 80,000 troops of the Allied forces were taken prisoners of war – including Britons, Indians, Australians and locals. Civilians were subjected to massacre, rape, forced prostitution, genocide, and general terror and humiliation, which had unfortunately become the common practice of the Japanese forces in territories that they occupied during WW2. People were screened systematically, and those having Chinese ethnicity or 'suspected' of carrying sentiment against Japanese imperialism were executed (Japan would later claim that it killed 'no more than' 6000, while Singapore estimated the number to be in the tens of thousands). Local informers helped the Japanese military police and were paid well. Singapore remained subjugated under Japan until the end of the war.

This event seems to have triggered the imagination of Gandhi and his followers in an extraordinary manner. The very next month, when senior British cabinet member Sir Stafford Cripps came forward with a renewed promise of a constituent assembly after the war, Gandhi brushed it aside (reportedly, by calling it 'a post-dated cheque on a crashing bank').

---

[1] Waheed Ahmad, *The Nation's Voice,* Vol.2, pp.575-576

This statement implied his assumption that the Allies were likely to lose the war. In April, Gandhi wrote in his widely followed journal:

> If the British left India to her fate as they had to leave Singapore, non-violent India would not lose anything... Whatever the consequences, therefore, to India, her real safety and Britain's too lie in orderly and timely British withdrawal from India... This presupposes Japan and other powers leaving India alone. If they do not, I should hope even then for wisdom to guide the principal parties [i.e. the Congress, the League and the Indian princes] to devise a scheme whereby they can act with one mind to face the new menace.[1]

If the British left India *as they had to leave Singapore,* really? Never mind if the people of India were to suffer like the people of Singapore, Gandhi and his Congress braced up for their greatest gamble: the 'Quit India' Movement, a ferocious revolt officially launched on 8 August, 1942.

The very next morning the Viceroy, in consultation with his Executive Council (which now included Indians), arrested Gandhi and hundreds of top-ranking leaders of the Congress.

Riots, terrorism and killings followed for a few months before gradually fizzling out in 1943. Gandhi was not released until 1944, and other leaders of the Congress remained imprisoned until much later. Thousands of party workers and activists arrested during the riots remained in prison until the end of the war. Although losses were enormous in terms of human life and public property, the movement never posed any serious threat to British rule from within India. From outside its borders however, the Congress had unleashed another demon.

Subhas Chandra Bose was two-times president of the Congress (in 1938 and 1939), before he was sacked for

---

[1] Gandhi, *The Collected Works,* Vol.82, pp.216-217

breaching the party discipline. In 1941, this early prototype of a James Bond villain escaped to Germany and attempted to persuade the Nazis to invade India. The Nazis helped him set up a propaganda centre in Berlin, Free India Centre; and a broadcasting service, Azad Hind Radio (Free India Radio) service.

Bose helped the Nazis brainwash Indian soldiers of the British army who had been taken as prisoners of war. Some three thousand were recruited in the Free India Legion of the Nazi army, pledging their loyalty to Hitler and Bose: 'I swear by God this holy oath that I will obey the leader of the German race and state, Adolf Hitler, as the commander of the German armed forces in the fight for India, whose leader is Subhas Chandra Bose.' Ultimately these Indians were drafted into the Waffen-SS (the combat branch of the Nazi party) to work for Heinrich Himmler, a boss of the Nazi party and one of the architects of the Jewish holocaust.[1]

Azad Hind Radio started broadcasting in October 1941, but Bose first spoke through it on 19 February 1942, rejoicing over the fall of Singapore that had happened four days earlier. Two more broadcasting services were added later. The transmissions were made initially from the Netherlands and afterwards from other locations.

These speeches give a fairly good idea of what the Congress, or at least Bose, meant by independence. As the Philippines, Malaya, Singapore and Burma fell to the Japanese forces, Bose declared that those countries had achieved freedom. Even more importantly, his speeches explicitly stated the same objectives of the Quit India Movement that Gandhi and the Congress leaders

---

[1] Some of the information about the Free India Legion presented here has been taken from the article 'Hitler's secret Indian army' by Mike Thomson last updated in the website of BBC News on 23 September 2004, and retrieved on 19 August 2022 from http://news.bbc.co.uk/2/hi/3684288.stm

Most other information about the wartime activities of Subhas Chandra Bose has been taken from *His Majesty's Opponent: Subhas Chandra Bose and India's Struggle Against Empire* by Sugata Bose

were conveying between the lines. Before and during that movement, Bose kept reassuring his Indian listeners that if the Nazis didn't conquer India, the Japanese would (of course, in order to bring it 'independence'). He kept congratulating Gandhi and his Congress for preparing the ground.

After meeting Bose face to face, Hitler arranged for him to reach Japan by a German submarine (which on its way there sank a passenger ship carrying Indians and Malayans, among others). In December 1941, while Bose was in Germany, the Japanese had formed the Burma Independence Army, which subsequently helped them conquer Burma between January and May 1942. Burma was then declared 'independent', only to have a puppet government while suffering from the tyranny of the Japanese occupation forces. Ironically, the Burma Independence Army, which had helped the Japanese liberate the country from the British, would later approach the British for help in liberating them from the Japanese.

Since India was also a British colony just like Burma, the Japanese wanted to repeat the same experiment there. Soon after taking Singapore, they had created an Indian National Army (INA), also called *Azad Hindu Fauj*. Commanded by an infamous Indian terrorist who had fled to Japan after attempting to assassinate an Indian Viceroy in 1912, this so-called army guarded the infamous Changi prison and carried out painful executions of the prisoners of war at the orders of the Japanese.

Bose visited Tokyo and pleaded for Prime Minister Tojo to attack India from the Japanese bases in Burma, before arriving in Singapore to take charge of the Indian National Army on 4 July 1943. The regiments were renamed after Gandhi and other presidents of the Congress, and a female regiment was added. The core strength of this army is estimated to have been more than fifty thousand at one time, comprising mostly Indian prisoners of war (just like the Free Indian Legion of the Nazi forces). It fought under the Japanese when they made a few raids into India, before being driven out by British Indian forces.

Afterwards the Japanese put the Indian National Army back to doing odd jobs for them in the occupied territories.

The Japanese also sponsored a Provisional Government of Free India (*Aarzi Hukumat-e-Azad Hind*), headed by Bose and launched as a government in exile from Singapore on 21 October 1943. It shifted to the Andaman and Nicobar Islands about two months later. The islands, formerly famed for housing the notorious British jail known as 'Kala Pani', had been captured by the Japanese. The islands remained in the control of the Japanese navy, while Bose served as a puppet ruler with a 'cabinet', a bank, and other paraphernalia of a state. He 'declared war' not only on Britain but also on the United States: 'You had an opportunity of helping us, but you did not do so. Now Japan is offering us help and we have reason to trust her sincerity.'

The loans he took from Japan were going to be repaid by India after it had been conquered by Japan. Fortunately, that did not happen. Japan surrendered, and Bose died in a plane crash soon afterwards on 18 August 1945.

The state established by Bose was a bona fide Axis state while it lasted. It was an Axis state because it had received international and diplomatic recognition from nine states of the Axis and pro-Axis powers, including each of the three major ones: Nazi Germany, the Empire of Japan and the Italian Social Republic (other states were the Independent State of Croatia, Thailand, the State of Burma, Manchukuo, the Second Philippine Republic and the puppet Wang Jingwei Government established by the Japanese in Eastern China). It was not recognized by any of the Allied powers.

Although the top-ranking leaders of the Congress remained imprisoned during the period of this state's existence, they gave it a backdated recognition in the very first meeting of the All-India Congress Committee conducted after their release (and this in addition signifies that the Gandhian Congress was a de facto Axis power during WW2).

'The Provisional Government is entitled to, and hereby claims, the allegiance of every Indian,' Bose had declared.1 But by what right? That question did not matter to him, or to the Congress.

3

At the time of presenting the Pakistan Resolution in March 1940, Jinnah reminded his people about the past betrayals by the British rulers and the Gandhian Congress, especially the British refusal to protect the minorities during Congress' rule. Then he said:

> We are now, therefore, very apprehensive and can trust nobody. I think it is a wise rule for every one not to trust anybody too much. Sometimes we are led to trust people, but when we find in actual experience that our trust has been betrayed, surely that ought to be sufficient lesson for any man not to continue his trust in those who have betrayed him... I therefore appeal to you, in all [the] seriousness that I can command, to organise yourselves in such a way that you may depend upon none except your own inherent strength. That is your only safeguard, and the best safeguard. Depend upon yourselves.[2]

He spent the next few years travelling across the Subcontinent, motivating the Muslims to achieve two things: (a) unity of thought; and (b) unity of action.

---

[1] 'Proclamation of Azad Hind Government'; Bhulabhai J. Desai, *I. N. A. Defence*, p.176
[2] Presidential address delivered at the Lahore session of the All-India Muslim League on 22 March 1940; Yusufi (ed.), *Speeches, Statements and Messages of the Quaid-e-Azam,,* p.1169-1170

Chapter 5: How India was liberated

Unity of thought meant that the entire society should agree on a common goal evolved by its members collectively, and not by one or a few individuals. The idea of Pakistan was an example. When Iqbal had first proposed it in 1930, he had said that he was only trying 'to read the Muslim mind.'[1] Likewise, when Jinnah was asked as to who was the author of Pakistan, his reply was, 'Every Mussalman.'[2]

Unity of action meant the power to transform the common idea into reality. It could only be achieved by gathering on the common platform of a national organization. The League had been winning almost every by-election on Muslim seats since 1937. In 1941, it demanded a general election, but that did not happen until five years later, once the war had ended.

By June 1945, Germany had surrendered, and both Mussolini and Hitler were dead. Japan was still fighting (it would eventually give up on 15 August and sign the instrument of surrender on 2 September, officially ending WW2). The victory of the Allies was certain in any case.

The League adhered to the policy it had announced in the early days of the war (already mentioned in the first section of this chapter). It had never discouraged ordinary Muslims from joining the war efforts. There were also no doubts in the minds of Muslims about the moral verdict of their leader: Jinnah had remained unequivocally critical of the Nazis and the Fascists; had persistently drawn similarities between them and his opponents, i.e. Gandhi and contemporary Hindu leaders; and had always described the position of the Muslims in India as being similar to that of the Allies in Europe, especially the British.

However, the League did not actively participate in the war efforts of the British because the announcement of Viceroy

---

[1] Presidential address delivered at the Allahabad session of the All-India Muslim League on 29 December 1930; Latif Ahmad Sherwani, *Speeches, Writings and Statements of Iqbal*, p.9

[2] The incident was mentioned by Jinnah in his speech at Aligarh, 8 March 1944; Yusufi, *op. cit.*, p.1841

Linlithgow on 8 August 1940 provided only a basic reassurance to the League without conceding the principle of Pakistan. It could not join the Viceroy's Executive Council or his war committees either, because the Viceroy failed to specify the position the League would have in those bodies relative to the Congress, if the Congress decided to join later.

Lord Wavell succeeded Linlithgow as the Viceroy of India in 1943, and he attempted to change this in June 1945. In a conference held at Simla, the summer capital of British India, he reassured the League that the Executive Council would include an equal number of representatives of Muslims and Caste Hindus (four each), along with representatives of some other communities. Members of the Congress Working Committee were released from imprisonment so that they could join the Simla Conference (but the remaining leaders of the Congress and other parties, and thousands of activists arrested in connection with the 'Quit India' riots were kept imprisoned until the surrender of their would-be master, Imperial Japan, in September). Practically forgetting everything it had said before, the Congress jumped at the suggestion and provided a long list of names for the new Executive Council.

Remembering the bitter lesson learnt in 1937, the League insisted that only Muslims nominated by the League should be included in the Executive Council. The Viceroy refused, but now he had to give in to the demand for general election. Among other things, the election would also test the League's claim to be the sole representative of the Indian Muslims.

The elections were held in the winter of 1945 and 1946. The League contested them on a single-point agenda: *Pakistan.* Jinnah's appeal to the Muslims was: 'You will not vote for personalities. The League candidate, even if he were a lamp post, you have to vote for him because he stands for Pakistan and your nation's freedom.'[1]

---

[1] Speech delivered at Allahabad, 14 February 1946; Yusufi, *op. cit.,* p.2191

Detailed results of the election have already been presented in the first chapter. To recap, the League received 75 percent of all the votes cast by the Muslims, securing 100 percent of the Muslim seats in the central assembly and some provinces, more than 80 percent in every other province except one – hence, 87 percent of the Muslim seats of all the legislatures combined. The claim that the League was the sole representative of the Indian Muslims was thus corroborated. The Congress received less than 5 percent of the votes cast by the Muslims.

The elected legislators of the Muslim League, some five hundred in all, assembled at the Muslim League Legislators' Convention held in Delhi on 7 and 8 April 1946. Unanimously they adopted the resolution frequently mentioned in this book as the Delhi Resolution of the League (at that time it was often called the Resolution of the Muslim League Legislators' Convention). The seven paragraphs of this resolution can be divided into three parts:

> a. *The rationale,* comprising the first five paragraphs, explained why the Muslim majority zones in the north-west and north-east of the Subcontinent should be made a separate sovereign state. Other than the fact that the Muslims were a nation, it also mentioned that a certain aspect of Hindu philosophy that had fostered and maintained a caste system in the past was now threatening 'to reduce Muslims, Christians and other minorities to the status of irredeemable helots, socially, and economically'.

> b. *The demand,* based on the Pakistan Resolution of 1940, was presented in the sixth paragraph: (a) the aforementioned zones should be made a sovereign state called Pakistan; (b) two constituent assemblies should be set up, respectively, for Pakistan and the rest of India (called 'Hindustan' in this resolution); (c) all rights of the minorities in both states should be protected in

consultation with them; and (d) the establishment of Pakistan should be promised without further delay.

   c. *The conviction* expressed in the last paragraph was that 'any attempt to impose a constitution on a united India basis or to force any interim arrangement at the centre contrary to the Muslim League demand will leave the Muslims no alternative but to resist such imposition by all possible means for their survival and national existence.'[1]

The elected legislators of the League, including Jinnah, took a pledge to 'willingly and unflinchingly carry out all the directions and instructions which may be issued by the All-India Muslim League in pursuance of any movement launched by it for the attainment of the cherished national goal of Pakistan.'[2] It was published in the Muslim newspapers with an appeal to every Muslim to take the same pledge.

    Since the rights of religious minorities had a fundamental significance in the idea of Pakistan, it needs to be remembered that according to the conventional political theory of Islam, which was followed by the top-ranking leaders of the League such as Iqbal, Jinnah and Liaquat Ali Khan, complete equality between Muslims and non-Muslims was possible. Any inequalities that might have existed in the past were understood to have been due to historical circumstances that had long ceased to exist. Non-Muslims could be and had been prime ministers of Muslim states, and this was reiterated by the leaders of the League on several occasions.

    This much was generally understood at that time. Soon after the adoption of the Delhi Resolution by the Muslim League Legislators' Convention, the Lahore-based Secretary of the Indian Social Congress, a prominent Christian Mrs K. L. Rallia Ram, wrote to Jinnah:

---

[1] Text of the resolution; Ahmad, *The Nation's Voice,* Volume 4, pp.653-657
[2] Text of the pledge; *ibid,* pp.671-672

I wondered whether we could organise a common front against this deadly foe, the Caste System, which threatens to engulf not only the Muslims but also other communities of India... Since the League Convention resolution is an open challenge not only to the Hindus, but also to the whole world that they are determined to resist all efforts to be yoked under a people whose social and economic machinery threatens the very existence of Muslims and others who differ in their way of life from Hindus, it is up to all these elements to unite under a common banner to expose this poisonous social structure, undemocratic in character. In order to strengthen the case of a separate homeland, the wicked implications of the caste system have to be thoroughly exposed... The Muslims, the Christians and other communities of India have to be told how the Hindu castes are a standing insult to all of them and an obstacle to national unity and common citizenship.[1]

4

In the meantime elections had also been held in the UK in July 1945.

The Labour Party secured 393 out of 640 seats, and 47.7 percent of the popular vote (this was considered a landslide victory). The party was generally known to be sympathetic towards the Congress, and the Prime Minister, Clement Attlee, was known to have opposed the separate electorates as a member of the Simon Commission (1927-1930).

---

[1] These are excerpts from a letter written by Mrs Ram to Jinnah on 29 May 1946, and included by Waheed Ahmad in *The Punjab Story: 1940-1947,* pp.431-2; Saleena Karim, *Secular Jinnah and Pakistan,* pp.354-355

During the elections in India in the winter of 1945-1946, the Labour government indicated its intention to send three senior members of the cabinet to India, in order to help Indian leaders arrive at an agreement over (a) the method or principles for framing the next constitution; (b) the setting up of a constituent assembly for the said purpose; and (c) the creation of an Interim Government including the major Indian political parties in the administration of the country, which would function until the new setup was ready.

In one of his statements about this Cabinet Mission in the House of Commons, Attlee hoped that India would choose to remain within the British Commonwealth, but if 'she elects for independence, in our view she has a right to do so. It will be for us to help to make the transition as smooth as possible.'[1]

This was a strange thing to say, because 'independence' in the sense of quitting the Commonwealth was a two-step process. A colony had to first acquire dominion status, which made it a free member of the Commonwealth. Only then it could opt out. The war-time Prime Minister Sir Winston Churchill, now the leader of the Opposition, criticized Attlee for a 'short-circuiting or telescoping of the normal procedure'.[2]

As a political stunt, the Congress had long been threatening this short-circuiting without ever intending to do so. Attlee's statement was therefore a wink to the Congress: *get your act together, we could be just fine.* This was emphasized by him as he further said, 'we cannot allow a minority to place a veto on the advance of the majority.'[3] Jinnah objected to this, and called it 'rope-walking'.[4]

Fifteen parliamentarians spoke on this subject in the House of Commons on 15 March, making it clear that the Labour,

---

[1] Ahmad, *The Nation's Voice,* Vol.5, p.689
[2] Churchill's speech in the House of Commons, 18 July 1946; Mitra (ed.), *Annual Indian Register,* Jul-Dec 1946, p.161
[3] Ahmad, *op. cit.*, p.690
[4] Ahmad, *The Nation's Voice,* Vol.4, p.520

Conservatives and the Unionists might have many differences among themselves but they were unanimous on one point: India must not be partitioned. The general sentiment of the House was summed by a Labour MP who described Pakistan 'as something with which no government in this country, and particularly no Labour government, could have anything at all to do.'[1]

The Cabinet Mission stayed in India from 24 March to 29 June and met several Indian leaders at Simla and Delhi – including the representatives of the League, the Congress, the Sikhs and the Depressed Classes. As the Indian leaders could not reach an agreement, the Mission suggested its own plan in two instalments, respectively announced on 16 May and 16 June:

5. the two zones of Muslim majority should retain central ties with the provinces of Hindu majority at least for ten years, and be free to leave afterwards if they wished; and an assembly should be elected through provincial legislatures to draft the constitution for this union;

6. almost immediately, the Viceroy should form an Interim Government consisting of the League, the Congress and a few other parties.

Not only did disputes arise over the meaning of the clauses in this plan, but the Congress appeared to reject it, and then later claimed to have accepted it.[2] The League, which had accepted the Plan,[3] felt betrayed as the Cabinet Mission suddenly left the country on 29 June and later tried to justify the position of the Congress.

What had the Cabinet Mission achieved? *Everything.* In maintaining their long rule over India, the British had always

---

[1] Ahmad, *The Nation's Voice,* Vol.5, p.700

[2] Resolutions passed by the Congress Working Committee on 26 June and 10 August 1946; *ibid,* pp.631-633, 637-638

[3] The League had accepted the Plan through resolutions passed by its Council on 6 June and its working committee on 26 June 1946; *ibid,* pp.558-561, 569-570

secured short-term leases sanctioned by the Parliament for ten to twenty years at a time (the charters granted to the East India Company, usually expiring after twenty years; the series of council acts introduced after India came directly under the Crown in 1858; and finally the constitutions of 1909, 1919 and 1935).

So, if those British politicians who wanted to continue ruling India were asked in 1946 what they really, really wanted, they would only have requested an extension of the British rule for ten to fifteen years. Such an extension could always be followed by another one, regardless of any promises made at the time, e.g. King George V had promised in 1919 that the next constitution would bring freedom to India, but that did not happen.

The Cabinet Mission secured such an extension by suggesting that a central assembly should start making the constitution while the dissident zones of the Subcontinent should wait for *ten years* before they could decide to leave (initially, the Cabinet Mission had attempted to make it a period of fifteen years). Obviously, some kind of British supremacy would be necessary throughout the said period, not only due to mistrust between the Muslims and the Hindus, but also because of the treaties between the Indian Princes and the Crown. So, the Cabinet Mission Plan was no different from any charter of the East India Company in its essence, although historical circumstances had required that it should be worded differently.

The Plan also ensured that the Gandhian Congress would actively support the British presence during the next ten years, to prevent the dissident provinces from leaving the union sooner. Indeed, the Congress supported the decision of the Viceroy to elect a constituent assembly in July and August, and also joined the Interim Government installed by him on 2 September.

The Interim Government was ironically operating under the same Government of India Act of 1919, which Gandhi had declared unacceptable even for a day and against which he had launched his campaign in 1920. Those pretences were now given up.

Nehru declared that this Interim Government overseen by a British Viceroy was the national government of India. He called it a cabinet. The constituent assembly inaugurated a little later was a sovereign body, according to him. That it was answerable to the British Parliament did not interfere with Nehru's concept of sovereignty. *So, this was the independence the Gandhian Congress had been harping about all this time?* It seemed so. 'Little things please little minds and you cannot turn a donkey into an elephant by calling it an elephant,' said Jinnah.[1]

5

Unlike the Congress' demand for a constituent assembly that necessitated British presence in India at least for another decade, the League's demand for Pakistan meant that the British should leave almost immediately, i.e. the peaceful transfer of power would require only a minimum of time, since British supervision would not be required for constitution-making. That could be done after they had left.

In the aftermath of the fiasco created by the Cabinet Mission, the Muslim League Council comprising representatives from all over British India met at Bombay from 27 to 29 July. Jinnah was asked to advise them about the next step, but he refused bluntly. 'I want you to take your own decision after ascertaining all the facts which I have placed before you,' he said. 'It is your bounded duty to decide what we should now do, for you are the parliament of the Muslim nation. The President and the Working Committee will carry out any policy laid down by you.'[2]

---

[1] 25 November 1946; *ibid,* p.415
[2] 28 July 1946; *ibid,* pp.152, 154

Some twenty-three speakers contributed to the debate, after which a resolution was adopted to say that there had been a breach of faith by the British government, and the Congress is bent upon establishing Caste Hindu *raj* in connivance with the British. Therefore, 'the time has come for the Muslim nation to resort to Direct Action to achieve Pakistan to assert their just rights, to vindicate their honour, and to get rid of the present British slavery and the contemplated future caste-Hindu domination.'[1] Jinnah then declared:

> What we have done today is the most historic act in our history. Never have we in the whole history of the League done anything except by constitutional methods. But now we are obliged and forced into this position. This day we bid goodbye to constitutional methods... 'If you seek peace, we do not want war, but if you want war, we will accept it unhesitatingly.'[2]

The last sentence was a quote from the Persian poet Firdausi.

16 August was chosen by the League as Direct Action Day. It was not for launching a direct action, the details of which were yet to be decided by the League. The purpose of Direct Action Day was to explain the meaning of direct action to the Muslim masses, and to inform them about the latest position of the League.

The day ended peacefully in most of India but not so in Calcutta, where it became the beginning of the 'Great Calcutta Killings' – four days of communal riots during which thousands of Muslims and Hindus got killed. In the subsequent weeks and months, violence began to erupt in many other areas. The worst hit was Bihar, where some thirty thousand Muslims were reportedly killed and up to fifteen thousand got displaced.

As already mentioned in the first chapter, this was by no means the beginning of communal violence in India. The

---

[1] Resolution adopted by the League Council on 29 July 1946; *ibid,* p. 566
[2] 29 July 1946; *ibid,* pp.165, 168

campaigns of Gandhi had also been accompanied by violence, very often along communal lines. Jinnah condemned the riots in clear terms, saying that any Muslims who commit violence would have 'only played into the hands of the enemies of the Muslim League', and 'must be dealt with according to law.'[1]

Initially the League refused to join the Interim Government. By mid-October, various political developments compelled it to take the five seats that had been allocated to it out of a total of fourteen, in which the Congress occupied six. The members nominated by Jinnah included a non-Muslim, the Scheduled Castes leader Jogindra Nath Mandal. His appointment in the quota of the League embarrassed the Congress but was welcomed by the Scheduled Castes, whom the Cabinet Mission had left feeling hurt as much as the Muslims.

The Constituent Assembly was due to be inaugurated on 7 December, and the League refused to join. The assembly was being set up on the basis of the Cabinet Mission Plan but the Congress had made it quite clear that it was going to disregard the Plan and proceed on the basis of a united India with a strong centre. This was unacceptable to the League, and besides, by withdrawing its conditional acceptance of the Cabinet Mission Plan it had reverted to its demand for a separate constituent assembly for Pakistan (as embodied in the Delhi Resolution adopted in April that year).

It was not possible for the British government to bypass this debacle. The Constituent Assembly comprised 389 seats (296 for the provinces of British India, and 93 for representatives of the Princely States). The seats allocated to the provinces of British India included 76 seats for Muslims, and the League held 73 of them. The absence of the League from the assembly meant that all the Muslim seats except three would remain empty.

There was no way the British government could explain this to the British public, or tell the British parliament that a

---

[1] 18 August 1946; *ibid,* p.215

constitution drafted by this assembly represented the whole of India. The three musketeers of the Cabinet Mission had thus ended up shooting themselves in the foot.

In order that Attlee would have the sweet pleasure of hearing 'No' with his own ears, Jinnah flew to London along with the Viceroy, Nehru, Liaquat Ali Khan, the Sikh representative Sardar Baldev Singh, and a small entourage.

A small round table conference, also called the London Talks, took place in early December. Jinnah had no need to say much. The actions of the Congress and the Cabinet Mission were speaking for him, louder than words. Attlee hoped that the League would cooperate with the Constituent Assembly with an assurance from the Congress it would faithfully follow the Cabinet Mission Plan. Instead Nehru repeated that the Congress had its own 'interpretation' of the Plan. Jinnah said only that if the Congress agreed to follow the Plan, he could call a meeting of the League Council after his return and see if the Council was willing to reconsider its position. As the talks ended on 6 December, Attlee had no choice but to state publicly:

> On the matter immediately in dispute, His Majesty's Government urge the Congress to accept the view of the Cabinet Mission in order that the way may be open for the Muslim League to reconsider their attitude… There has never been any prospect of success for the Constituent Assembly except upon the basis of an agreed procedure. Should a constitution come to be framed by a Constituent Assembly in which a large section of the Indian population had not been represented, His Majesty's Government could not of course contemplate—as the Congress have stated they would not contemplate—forcing such a constitution upon any unwilling parts of the country.[1]

---

[1] Text of the statement; *ibid,* p.1013

This is when the British public started taking an active interest, as Jinnah had long wanted.

He sat in the Distinguished Strangers' Gallery of the Parliament on the first two days of a heated debate on India that took place from 11 to 13 December[1] (by then, Nehru had left for Delhi, where the Constituent Assembly was inaugurated on 9 December).

Churchill roasted one of the three members of the Cabinet Mission, accused the Labour Party of playing into the hands of the Congress, and alleged that by inviting Nehru to form an Interim Government it had facilitated a series of massacres unparalleled in India since the Mutiny of 1857. He asked the Labour Government whether it considered the sessions of the Constituent Assembly in Delhi to be valid when the Muslim League was not attending them: 'if a bride or a bridegroom fails to turn up in the church, the result is not called a unilateral wedding.'[2]

Churchill had not cared enough about the minorities of India while he was in power, he was as much committed to the idea of a united India as anybody else in Britain, and he was an imperialist to the core. But his penchant for greatness, his own and his nation's, compelled him to blurt out what others had dreaded to contemplate.

'In all this confusion, uncertainty and gathering storm,' he said, there were three proverbial choices before the British Parliament: (a) just pack up, and leave India to its fate; (b) partition India between the Hindus and the Muslims; or (c) use the British troops to enforce the Caste Hindu domination upon the Muslims, the Scheduled Castes and other minorities of India.

Churchill was condemned by most of those who spoke after him. Even his own Conservative Party seemed reluctant to support his views at this point. Yet one of the Labour MPs who had assisted the Cabinet Mission ended up saying:

---

[1] For itinerary of Jinnah's engagements in UK, see footnote on *ibid,* pp.ciii-civ

[2] Mitra, *Indian Annual Register,* Jul-Dec 1946, p.310

We must say clearly and unequivocally to India that, on a certain fixed date, we are going to leave India with our troops, with our officials, and with any British residents who wish to go with us. We must announce that date before the administrative machinery has completely crumbled in our hands. That date, I would suggest, should certainly not be more than twelve months ahead. We cannot allow British troops to be dragged into either side in a civil war.[1]

This shift in the British public opinion compelled the Congress to increase its political emotional blackmail, and hence Nehru groused in the Constituent Assembly at Delhi that 'at this psychological moment in India's history when we wanted, when we hungered for messages of cheer, friendship and cooperation from all over the world, and more especially from England... I came back without any message of cheer, but with a large measure of disappointment.'[2]

Gripped with panic at the thought of losing the aid of the British bayonets, the Constituent Assembly ended up violating several conditions that had been laid down by the Cabinet Mission, while the Congress Working Committee and the All India Congress Committee made desperate attempts to prove that they were not deviating from the Plan.[3]

These contradictory words and actions of the Congress were analysed by the Working Committee of the League in a meeting held from 29 January to 2 February. It was decided that the Congress had failed to provide the necessary assurance. Therefore there was no reason for the League to reconsider its

---

[1] This was Maj. Woodrow Wyatt; *ibid,* p.312.
[2] 13 December 1946; *Selected Works of Jawaharlal Nehru: Second Series,* Vol.1, p.249
[3] Resolutions adopted by the All India Congress Committee on 26 December 1946 and the Congress Working Committee on 6 January 1947; Ahmad, *The Nation's Voice,* Vol.5, pp.624-626, 672-677

rejection of the Cabinet Mission's plan. The League was not going to the Constituent Assembly.[1]

6

Thus the League ended up taking four out of the five steps of the 'freedom through disobedience' strategy of C. R. Das (which Iqbal had acknowledged as his own spiritual principle of *khudi*).

The League had (a) provided complete reassurance to the minorities; (b) contested election on a single-point agenda; (c) swept the polls; and (d) not cooperated with the assembly. If Das had been right, and if Iqbal's philosophy was sound, the next thing to happen would be the independence of India. And it was.

On 20 February 1947, Attlee made the announcement which has been mentioned earlier in this book: the British were going to leave India no later than June 1948. Their specifying a date not even eighteen months away indicated that they meant what they said.

How this decision was subsequently implemented is irrelevant to the main topic of this book. Once the decision was made, it had to be implemented one way or another. However, five implications must be taken into account.

Firstly, the rationale provided by Attlee was consistent with the point of view of the original Congress and the League. As already mentioned, they believed that although many British politicians were playing dirty tricks to delay the independence of India, the spirit of the British policy was sound and reliable. And this is how Attlee started his historic statement:

> It has long been the policy of successive British Governments to work towards the realization of self-government in India. In pursuance of this policy an

---

[1] Text of the resolution; *ibid*, pp.576-586

increasing measure of responsibility has been devolved on Indians, and today the Civil Administration and the Indian Armed Forces rely to a very large extent on Indian civilians and officers. In the constitutional field the Acts of 1919 and 1935 passed by the British Parliament each represented a substantial transfer of political power. In 1940 the Coalition Government recognized the principle that Indians should themselves frame a new Constitution for a fully autonomous India, and in the offer of 1942 they invited them to set up a Constituent Assembly for this purpose as soon as the war was over.

His Majesty's Government believe this policy to have been right and in accordance with sound democratic principles.[1]

By implication, it also became clear that the Gandhian Congress and their sideshows had played no part in the process.

Each and every constitutional step that had led to the independence of India according to this statement was a step resisted by Gandhi and his associates: (a) the Act of 1919 was opposed through the campaign of 1920-1922; (b) the drafting of the Act of 1935 had been opposed through the famous Salt March, and the campaigns of 1930-1931 and 1933; (c) the 1940 announcement of the Coalition Government (the 'August Offer' mentioned earlier in this chapter) had been spurned with the campaign of 'individual satyagraha'; (d) the offer of 1942 (the Cripps' Proposals) had been answered with the 'Quit India' movement.

This is all the more significant because the statement was coming from the Labour Government, whose sympathy for the Gandhian Congress was no secret. If it had been possible at all to

---

[1] The statement appears in the British Parliamentary Debates [Hansard], 20 February 1947, House of Commons, Vol.433, cols.1396-1404; Waheed Ahmad (ed.), *The Nation's Voice*, Vol.5, pp.1105-1108. On the official website, https://hansard.parliament.uk, the debate appears as dated 10 February 1947, which is a mistake (retrieved 19 August 2022).

give any credit to Gandhi and his associates, nobody would have been more eager to do it than Attlee and his colleagues, but the facts did not support them.

Secondly, although Attlee and the Labour Government would have been the last people on earth to admit that it was the League who actually forced them to quit India, facts compelled them to do so. They still refrained from taking any names, but after explaining the failure of the Cabinet Mission (in paragraphs 2-5), it had to be admitted (in paragraphs 6-7) that the main reason for quitting was that the League had refused to join the Constituent Assembly:

> It is with great regret that His Majesty's Government find that there are still differences among Indian Parties which are preventing the Constituent Assembly from functioning as it was intended that it should. It is of the essence of the plan that the Assembly should be fully representative.
>
> His Majesty's Government desire to hand over their responsibility to authorities established by a Constitution approved by all Parties in India in accordance with the Cabinet Mission's plan, but unfortunately there is at present no clear prospect that such a Constitution and such authorities will emerge. The present state of uncertainty is fraught with danger and cannot be indefinitely prolonged. His Majesty's Government wish to make it clear that it is their definite intention to take the necessary steps to effect the transference of power into responsible Indian hands by a date not later than June, 1948.[1]

Although the Labour Government would continue expressing its preference for a united India, the likelihood of Pakistan had also to be conceded in the tenth paragraph of the statement:

> His Majesty's Government will have to consider to whom the powers of the Central Government in British India

---

[1] *Ibid.*

should be handed over, on the same date, whether as a whole to some form of Central Government for British India or in some areas to the existing Provincial Governments, or in such other way as may seem most reasonable and in the best interests of the Indian people.[1]

Such other way as may seem most reasonable? That was Pakistan, without being named. This also proved what Jinnah had been saying since 1940, that India would gain independence only *after* the British had accepted the demand for Pakistan, and not before. This conviction had also been incorporated in the Delhi Resolution of the League Convention in April 1946, and the Pledge taken by the Muslims on that occasion.

Thirdly, these historical facts make it obvious that Jinnah is the founder of the country that now exists by the name of India – not the India that had existed before 15 August 1947, but the one that came into existence on that date. Of course, Jinnah is also the creator of Pakistan, but that fact is already recognized. What is yet to be understood is that he not only created Pakistan but also the other country, which is now known as the Republic of India or Bharat (it was initially called the Union of India, from 1947 to 1950).

If the founder of a country is someone who either liberated it from foreign rule, or shaped its boundaries, or calibrated it to its existing position with respect to other countries, Jinnah did all these things for the existing state of India.

We have seen that he liberated the Subcontinent from the British rule. Gandhi and his associates did not. The Subcontinent thus liberated by Jinnah which also includes present-day India.

The boundaries of modern India, which do not include Pakistan and Bangladesh, were also shaped by the success of the movement led by Jinnah.

These boundaries had never been contemplated by Gandhi and his associates. Even at the time of accepting the Partition

---

[1] *Ibid.*

Plan on 3 June, Nehru had said, 'The India of geography, of history and traditions, the India of our minds and our hearts cannot change.'[1] This statement of Nehru was further elaborated by the All India Congress Committee when it endorsed the Partition Plan a few days later:

> Geography and the mountains and the seas fashioned India as she is and no human agency can change that shape or come in the way of her final destiny. Economic circumstances and the insistent demands of international affairs make the unity of India still more necessary. The picture of India we have learnt to cherish will remain in our minds and hearts. The All-India Congress Committee earnestly trusts that when present passions have subsided, India's problems will be viewed in their proper perspective and the false doctrine of two nations in India will be discredited and discarded by all.[2]

The resolution fails to acknowledge the boundaries of present-day India, as it confuses at least two other sovereign states as integral parts of that country.

Fourthly, Jinnah was the first non-white governor-general in any dominion of the Commonwealth. The office represents the Crown, and in all essential respects it holds the same position in relation to the administration of public affairs in the dominion as is held by the King in Great Britain. Jinnah became the first non-white person to hold this office, as the Muslim League nominated him the Governor-General of Pakistan in July 1947 (the Congress had nominated Lord Mountbatten for the same position in the Indian Union), and he subsequently took the oath on 15 August 1947.

One interesting development in this regard was the form of the oath. The governors-general of dominions usually take two oaths. The oath of allegiance in those days was, 'I do swear that I

---

[1] Nehru's statement 3 June 1947; Ahmed, *The Nation's Voice,* Volume 5, p.477
[2] Resolution of the All India Congress Committee, 15 June 1947; *ibid,* p.400

will be faithful and bear true allegiance to His Majesty King George VI, his heirs and successors, according to law. So help me God'. In the oath of office it was said, 'I do swear that I will well and truly serve His Majesty King George VI in the office of the Governor-General. So help me God'. The names of the person and the dominion used to be inserted accordingly.

The Secretary of State suggested the same form of oath to Mountbatten on 24 July, to be taken by him and Jinnah on the morning of independence.[1] Five days later, Mountbatten suggested an alteration, adding allegiance to the constitutions of the respective countries *after* allegiance to the king and his successors in the oath of allegiance; and omitting allegiance to the king and his successors from the oath of office.[2]

After approval from London, this altered form was sent to Jinnah. He did not like it and presented a new form for himself on 10 August, which was presented to the King two days later and received approval soon afterwards. This new form of oath, which Jinnah used for assuming office on 15 August, was:

> I, Muhammad Ali Jinnah, do solemnly affirm true faith and allegiance to Constitution of Pakistan as by law established, and that I will be faithful to His Majesty King George VI, his heirs and successors, in office of Governor General of Pakistan.[3]

This form of oath, subsequently used by all governors-general who succeeded Jinnah in Pakistan until 1956 (when Pakistan became a republic), was a 'denial of allegiance to the British Sovereign' according to one of the ablest judges of the Commonwealth, Justice R. A. Cornelius. He wrote in a historical judgment in 1955:

---

[1] Mansergh, *Transfer of Power,* Vol.12, p.311
[2] *Ibid,* p.402
[3] *Ibid,* p.647

The first such act was performed by the first Governor-General of Pakistan, the late Quaid-e-Azam Muhammad Ali Jinnah. When the time came for him to take the oath upon assuming office as Governor-General of Pakistan, he refused to accept the earlier form which required the Governor-General to bear 'true faith and allegiance to His Majesty' and thereupon, by agreement with the British Sovereign, the oath which he took and which, his successors after him have taken, requires that he should bear true allegiance to the Constitution and be faithful to His Majesty. Nothing can indicate more clearly that appointment at the hands of the British Sovereign to the office of the Governor-General of Pakistan is accepted by the Governor-General of this country in a form vastly different from that which the Governors-General of the other Dominions are required to accept. In the case of these latter Governors-General, they swear 'true faith and allegiance to the British Sovereign.' That imports of necessity a disparity of position and acceptance of servitude. The Governor-General of Pakistan, when he swears to 'be faithful to the British Sovereign' cannot be thought to accept any inferiority of position, much less of servitude in the feudal sense appropriate to the conception of royalty. At the highest it is an undertaking of loyalty on equal terms, and entirely appropriate to acceptance of the British Sovereign not as a Queen, but as a symbolic Head of the Commonwealth.[1]

Last but not the least, in light of all the facts presented here, Jinnah was the person who played a more significant role than anybody else in transforming the greatest empire of history into a true Commonwealth.

---

[1] Federation of Pakistan vs. Maulvi Tamizuddin, PLD 1955 Federal Court 240. Text of the judgment from https://pbbarcouncil.com (retrieved 19 August 2022).

In the first place, he liberated the Subcontinent and thus brought the Indian Union and Pakistan into the Commonwealth as the first two dominions that represented people who did not have racial affinity with Britain. Moreover, the single act of defiance through which he brought down the biggest empire in history, and rebooted it as a true Commonwealth, was his refusal to send his party to a constituent assembly that did not represent his people. It is not possible to conceive a more democratic foundation for the future. In the words of King George VI, addressed to the people of Pakistan on the occasion when power was being transferred to them:

> In thus achieving your independence by agreement, you have set an example to all freedom-loving people throughout the world.
>
> I know that I can speak for all sections of opinion within the British Commonwealth when I say that their support will not fail you in upholding democratic principles. I am confident that the statesmanship and the spirit of cooperation which have led to the historic developments you are now celebrating will be the best guarantee of your future happiness and prosperity.
>
> Great responsibilities lie ahead of you and your leaders. May the blessings of the Almighty sustain you in all your future tasks.[1]

---

[1] Constituent Assembly of Pakistan, *Debates,* 14 August 1947, p.49

Appendix

The following is the toast offered by Jinnah as Governor-General designate to His Majesty King George VI at an official banquet held in Karachi on 13 August 1947. Since Jinnah was in the unique position of representing, not only the Muslims of the Subcontinent and the upcoming state of Pakistan, but also the British sovereign himself, the summary of the British rule offered here must be treated as the official perspective of all three entities. Of course, it also represents the point of view held by the pioneers of the Indian National Congress. As such, it deserves to be treated as the mainstream narrative (even though it was not shared by Gandhi and his associates).

Your Excellency, Your Highness, and Ladies and Gentlemen, I have great pleasure in proposing a toast to His Majesty the King.

This is one of the most momentous and unique occasions. Today, we are on the eve of complete transfer of power to the people of India, and there will emerge and establish two Independent Sovereign Dominions of Pakistan and Hindustan on the appointed day, the 15th of the August, 1947.

This decision of His Majesty's Government will mark the fulfilment of the great ideal which was set forth by the formation of Commonwealth with the avowed object to make all nations and countries which formed part of the British Empire, self-governing and independent states, free from the domination of any other nation.

Since the assumption of the reign of the Government of India by Queen Victoria, a great and good Queen, by the Proclamation and the very Act that was enacted for the assumption of power and authority of the British Crown and Parliament, it was made clear that it will be the deep concern and definite objective of the British Nation to lead India ultimately to the goal of its becoming self-governing and Independent State.

In the pursuit of that policy since the days of Macaulay there never was any question about the principle, but there remained always the question of how and when.

In that process during the reign of four generations of the British Crown there were controversies and differences of opinion as to the pace for realization of Freedom and Independence. There have been many acts of commission and omission, but at the same time we cannot help recognizing that the British genius and those Britishers who ruled India for over a century did so to the best of their judgement and have left their marks in many spheres of life and especially the judicial system, which has been the greatest bulwark and safeguard for the rights and liberties of the people.

Today, it falls to the lot of King George the Sixth, the good fortune of fulfilling the promise and the noble mission with which his great-grandmother assumed the reigns of this subcontinent nearly a century ago.

The reign of King George the Sixth will go down in history by the performance of this act voluntarily of transferring power and handing over the government of India which was rightly characterized as the brightest jewel in the British Empire, and by establishing two Sovereign Dominions of Pakistan and Hindustan.

Such voluntary and absolute transfer of power and rule by one nation over others is unknown in the whole history of the world. It is the translation and the realization of the Great Ideal of Commonwealth which now has been effected and hence both Pakistan and Hindustan have remained members of Commonwealth, which shows how truly we appreciate the high and noble ideal by which the Commonwealth has been and will be guided in the future.

Appendix

Here I would like to say, Your Excellency Lord Mountbatten, how much we appreciate your having carried out wholeheartedly the policy and the principle that was laid down by the plan of 3rd June and the Indian Independence Act which was passed by the British Parliament and received the assent of His Majesty the King on the 10th of July with grace, dignity and great ability. You are the last Viceroy of India, but Pakistan and Hindustan will always remember you, and your name will remain cherished not only in the history of these two Dominions but will find a place in the history of the world, as one who performed his task and duties magnificently.

Before I conclude, let me mark our sense of deep appreciation of the Prime Minister, Mr. Attlee, and His Majesty's Government and the British Parliament, and above all, the British nation who enthusiastically and wholeheartedly helped and supported the policy enunciated by His Majesty's Government that the people of India should be free, and that the only solution of India's constitutional problem was to divide it into Pakistan and Hindustan.

This task has now been accomplished.

There lies in front of us a new chapter and it will be our endeavour to create and maintain goodwill and friendship with Britain and our neighbouring dominion Hindustan along with other sister nations so that we all together may make our greatest contribution for the peace and prosperity of the world.

And now Ladies and Gentlemen, I propose the health of His Majesty, King George the Sixth.[1]

---

[1] Khursheed Ahmad Khan Yusufi (ed.), *Speeches, Statements & Messages of the Quaid-e-Azam,* pp.2606-2609

References

A correspondent lately returned from India. 'Deathbed of the Indian Empire' in *The Round Table*. Vol. 37, no. 147 (1947), pp.231-236

All-India Conference of the Moderate Party. [*n.d.*]. *Report of the Proceedings of the First Session of the All-India Conference of the Moderate Party held at Bombay in the Empire Theatre on the 1ˢᵗ and 2ⁿᵈ November 1918.* Bombay: The Times Press

Ahmad, Waheed (Ed.).1992-2003. *Quaid-i-Azam Muhammad Ali Jinnah: The Nation's Voice; Speeches and statements* (in 7 volumes). Karachi: Quaid-i-Azam Academy

Bamford, P. C. 1925. *Histories of the Non-Co-operation and Khilafat Movements.* Delhi: Government of India Press

Bose, Sugata. 2011. *His Majesty's Opponent: Subhas Chandra Bose and India's Struggle Against Empire.* Cambridge, Massachusetts: The Belknap Press of Harvard University Press

Brooke, Rupert. 1915. *1914 and other Poems.* London: Sidgwick & Jackson, Ltd.

Constituent Assembly of Pakistan, *Debates.* Retrieved from https://na.gov.pk on 30 August 2016

Desai, Bhulabhai J. [*n.d.*]. *I. N. A. Defence.* Delhi: I. N. A. Defence Committee

Das, C. R. [Chittaranjan]. 1921. *India for Indians.* Madras: Ganesh & Co.

—. 1922. *Freedom Through Disobedience.* Madras: Arka Publishing house

Follett, Mary Parker (with Introduction by Lord Haldane. 1923. *The New State: Group Organization the Solution of Popular Government.* London: Longmans, Green and Co.

Gandhi, Mohandas Karamchand. *The Collected Works of Mahatma Gandhi* (Electronic Book in 98 volumes). New Delhi: Publications Division Government of India, 1999, 98 volumes [Retrieved from www.gandhiashramsevagram.org in August 2022]

Government of India. 1943. *Congress Responsibility for the Disturbance 1942-43.* Delhi: Government of India Press

Imperial Conference 1926. *Summary of Proceedings.* Ottawa: F. A. Acland

Indian National Congress. [*n.d.*]. *Proceedings of the First Indian National Congress held at Bombay on the 28th, 29th and 30th December 1885.* Bombay: [*Publisher not mentioned*]

—. [*n.d.*]. *Report of the Thirty-first Indian National Congress held at Lucknow on the 26th, 28th, 29th and 30th December 1916.* Lucknow: The Reception Committee at Lucknow

—. [*n.d.*]. *The Indian National Congress 1930-34: being the resolutions passed by the Congress, the All India Congress Committee and the Working Committee during the period between Jan. 1930 to Sep. 1934. Some important statements and other documents of the period are also given.* Allahabad: All India Congress Committee

—. [*n.d.*]. *Report of the 52nd Indian National Congress Tripuri (Dt. Jubbulpore), Mahakoshal, 1939.* Tripuri: All India Congress Committee

—. 1933. *A History of the Hindu-Muslim Problem in India: From the Earliest Contacts upto Its Present Phase, With Suggestions for Its Solution. Being the report of the committee appointed by the Indian National Congress (Karachi Session 1931) to enquire into the Cawnpore Riots of March 1931.* Allahabad: Cawnpore Riots Enquiry Committee

Indian Round Table Conference. *Proceedings of Sub-Committees.* Volume 3—Sub-Committee No.3 (Minorities). Calcutta: Government of India Central Publication Branch

Iqbal, Dr Sir Muhammad. 1934. *The Reconstruction of Religious Thought in Islam.* London: Oxford University Press

Iqbal, Dr Javid; Khurram Ali Shafique (Ed.). 2006. *Stray Reflections – the private notebook of Muhammad Iqbal. Also include: 'Stray Thoughts'.* Lahore: Iqbal Academy Pakistan

Ispahani, M. A. H. (Ed.). 1976. *M.A. Jinnah-Ispahani Correspondence 1936-1948.* Karachi: Forward Publications Trust

Joshi, Vijaya Chandra. [*n.d.*]. *Lala Lajpat Rai: Writings and Speeches. Volume Two: 1920-1928.* Delhi: University Publishers

Karim, Saleena. 2017. *Secular Jinnah and Pakistan: What the Nation Doesn't Know (Revised and Enlarged).* Nottingham: Libredux

Kipling, Rudyard. 1892. *Barrack-Room Ballads and other Verses.* Leipzig: Heinemann and Balestier Ltd. London

Macaulay, T.B. 1853. *Speeches of the Right Honorable T. B. Macaulay – corrected by himself* (in 2 volumes). Leipzig: Bernhard Tauchnitz

Mansergh, Nicholas. *Et al.* 1970-1983. *The Transfer of Power* (in 12 volumes). London: Her Majesty's Stationery Office

Masani, R. P. 1939. *Dadabhai Naoroji – The Grand Old Man of India.* London: George Allen & Unwin Ltd.

Metcalf, Henry C.; and L. Urwick. 2003. *Dynamic Administration: The Collected Papers of Mary Parker Follett.* London: Routledge

Mitra, Nripendra Nath Mitra (ed.). *The Indian Annual Register Jan-Jun 1937.* Calcutta: N. N. Mitra

—. *The Indian Annual Register Jul-Dec 1946.* Calcutta: N. N. Mitra

—. *The Indian Annual Register Jan-Jun 1947.* Calcutta: N. N. Mitra

Nehru, Jawaharlal. 1984-2017. *Selected Works of Jawaharlal Nehru: Second Series* (in 85 volumes). New Delhi: Jawaharlal Nehru Memorial Fund

Nichols, Beverley. 1944. *Verdict on India.* London: Jonathan Cape

Parekh, Chunilal Lallubhai (Ed.). 1887. *Essays, Speeches, Addresses and Writings (On Indian Politics) of the Hon'ble Dadabhai Naoroji.* Bombay: Caxton Printing Works

Pirzada, Syed Sharifuddin (Ed.). 1984-1986. *The Collected Works of Quaid-e-Azam Mohammad Ali Jinnah* (in 3 volumes). Karachi: East and West Publishing Company

Rahman, Hafizur (Ed.). 1929. *Report of the All-India Muslim Conference held at Delhi on 31st December 1928 and 1st January 1929.* Aligarh: Hafizur Rahman

Razzaqi, Shahid Hussain (Ed.). 2003. *Discourses of Iqbal.* Lahore: Iqbal Academy Pakistan

Rogers, James E. Thorold (ed.).1868. *Speeches on Questions of Public Policy by John Bright MP* (in 2 volumes). London: Macmillan & Co.

Shqfique, Khurram Ali Shafique. 2018. *Jinnah: The Case for Pakistan.* Nottingham: Libredux

Sherwani, Latif Ahmad; ed. 1995. *Speeches, Writings and Statements of Iqbal.* Iqbal Academy Pakistan, Lahore

Tanvir, Hina (retold). 2006. *Javidnama* (Junior Edition). Lahore: Iqbal Academy Pakistan

Yusufi, Khurshid Ahmad Khan (ed.). 1996. *Speeches, Statements and Messages of the Quaid-e-Azam* (in 4 volumes). Lahore: Bazm-i-Iqbal

Persian

Iqbal, Dr Sir Muhammad. 1927. *Zabur-i-Ajam.* Lahore: [self-published by the author]

—. 1932. *Javid Nama.* Lahore: [self-published by the author]

Urdu

Burney, Dr S. M. H. 1992-1998. *Kuliyat Makateeb-e-Iqbal* (in 4 volumes). Delhi: Urdu Academy

Panipati, Sheikh Muhammad Ismail. 2009. *Khutbat-i-Sir Syed.* Lahore: Majlis Taraqqi-i-Adab

About the author

Khurram Ali Shafique has thrice received the Presidential Iqbal Award for his ground-breaking research. He has authored several books, articles and papers, and has also delivered talks at international forums including the universities of Cambridge, Oxford and Warwick in UK, and at various conferences and seminars in Iran, Mauritius, Hong Kong and India. He was also a research consultant with Iqbal Academy Pakistan from 2003 to 2015.

He is the pioneer of online courses in Iqbal Studies, which he offers internationally from Marghdeen, the online Iqbal Studies Centre founded by him in 2011. He is also the writer, producer and director of *Jinnah: The True Story* (2020).

He started his career as an educationist, receiving training as a trainer from Jordanhill College of Education, Strathclyde University, Glasgow (UK) in 1990. Subsequently, he also wrote screenplays for television, mostly adaptations of Persian classics from Nezami Ganjavi and Ferdowsi to the present-day settings.

His most acclaimed printed work includes *Iqbal: An Illustrated Biography* (2006), *The Republic of Rumi: A Novel of Reality* (2007), *Iqbal: His Life and Our Times* (2014), *Waheed Murad: His Life and Our Times* (2015), and a series of authentic biographies of Iqbal in Urdu, including *Iqbal Ki Manzil* (2019).

His official website is located at Marghdeen.com and his YouTube channel is youtube.com/c/Khurramsdesk.